"Ruth Keidel Clemens' memoir, *A Quest for Purpose,* is a fascinating first-person account of the foundations of her life-long pursuit of meaning. Through a series of stories, 'touch points' from her life, she traces the roots of a rich legacy of resilience and determination that led to a long and productive leadership role as MCC's International Program Director. Her descriptions of missionary life growing up as an MK through the chaotic days of Congo's post-Independence are particularly informative and inspiring. Readers are challenged to consider their own 'calling' to live a purposeful life."

—John B. Franz, Ph.D.,
Professor Emeritus, California State University,
Fresno, author of *The Mabamba Return*

"Ruth shares with the reader the twists and turns in her life, concluding that God is much bigger than we are. With that understanding, she encourages us to look around with anticipation and expectancy; observe with gratitude what God is already doing in your community and in the world. I encourage you to read her book through that lens and consider how it applies to your own life. You will find yourself deeply encouraged."

—Brad Graber,
Co-founder of Hope for Congo

"Ruth Keidel Clemens crafts a poignant story of human drama spanning five decades while engaging in cultural immersion across three continents. From 'eating gasoline soup' to living through the Simba rebellion, from assisting Cambodian refugees who survived Pol Pot's 'Reign of Terror' to helping Muslim asylum-seekers in Baltimore, Clemens retells a fascinating life story with wit and insight. Not many have had a parallel global exposure or this impact on so many lives. This is an engrossing and enjoyable read."

—Tim Bertsche,
Pastor and Missionary

"The through-line of Ruth Keidel Clemens's memoir is her passion for discovering—and living into—a purpose-filled life. Believing that all have a 'function' (a unique meaning of the word was picked up from English learners in post-war Cambodia), Clemens credits her passion to the influences of her parents, who persevered as missionaries in war-torn pre- and post-independence Congo; and to her grandparents and great-grandparents—especially the resilience and determined strength of her grandmother who persevered while losing most of her family, one after another, to the 'plague'. Clemens paints vibrant and kaleidoscopic pictures of a life shaped by the unique influences of growing up as an 'MK' (Missionary Kid) and of a career that often crossed national and personal boundaries. Her purpose in the telling of the 'twists and turns' in her journey is to inspire others to find their own purpose and meaning in life; lives that are dedicated to creating a more compassionate and peace-filled world and that celebrate the richness of differences. Her story is inspirational and recommended reading!"

—John Yoder,
International Consultant and Lecturer,
Retired Professor, Academic Dean, and
Chief Academic Officer,
author of *Between: An Amish Boy's Odyssey*

"In current turbulent tides of change, domestic and world conflicts and dominance politics, Ruth Keidel Clemens' memoir reverberates with a way through the fracturing to a footing grounded in honesty, humility and showing up to serve in some of the world's worst red zones. This five-senses, coming of age story of a little American girl growing up in the Democratic Republic of Congo brings the reader along as she flees two wars by the time she's eight, yet still is drawn to her African home. A near death experience in the jungle between her junior and senior year of high school crystallizes for her that life must have a purpose. At the same time she awakens to the fact of her own privilege, when a village boy caught in the same situation, dies a torturous death. Ruth's willingness to own the tension of colonial privilege, while also accepting the responsibility of leadership in rebuilding through some of the worst aftermath of America's wars, makes this a must-read. Keidel Clemens' strength is her credibility won through a lifetime of choosing courageous presence and simplicity in forging peace."

—Charity Schellenberg,
Author, Educator, Entrepreneur

A QUEST FOR PURPOSE

From Illinois to Congo, Cambodia and Beyond

RUTH KEIDEL CLEMENS

LUCIDBOOKS

A Quest for Purpose: From Illinois to Congo, Cambodia and Beyond

Published by Lucid Books in Houston, TX
www.LucidBooks.com

ISBN: 978-1-63296-960-6
eISBN: 978-1-63296-961-3

Special Sales: Most Lucid Books titles are available in special quantity discounts. Custom imprinting or excerpting can also be done to fit special needs. Contact Lucid Books at Info@LucidBooks.com

These stories are dedicated to my four children,
Carla, Chris, Andy and Hana,
who heard about many of my Congo escapades
at bedtime.

Contents

Special Thanks

Many thanks to my parents, Levi and Eudene Keidel, who shared many of these stories throughout my life, and to Levi for his photographic eye. Special thanks to Jonathan Clemens, who provided critical feedback, support and encouragement throughout this project; and to Hana Clemens for her input and advice on the theme and throughline of this book. RKC

Preface

"Have you read *The Poisonwood Bible*?" (P1)

That is a question people often ask me when I tell them I grew up in the Democratic Republic of Congo. "Yes, I've read it," I say, "but it doesn't reflect my personal experience." Missionaries are normal, flawed human beings, but most of them, in my experience, have a positive motivation to spread goodness in the world.

Growing up as a missionary kid in Africa felt like a privilege to me. How many people can learn about other cultures in everyday life, travel to remote places of intricate beauty, or learn another language or two as a child?

Levi and Ruth harvesting pineapple

My parents' strong sense of purpose in life was foundational in shaping who I am. What life experiences gave them a sense of resilience, determination, and motivation to take risks to improve the lives of the Congolese people? The stories in this book attempt to address that question.

Yes, there were many nuances and complexities to the missionary endeavor. In the early years, my parents' presence in Congo was dependent on the colonial structures. I will attempt to illustrate how that colonial history played out in our lived experience as a family and missionary community.

Through the telling of these stories from life in Congo and beyond, I hope you will find encouragement to reflect on your own touchpoints in life and how they have impacted you as an adult. I hope that through these stories you will find ways to live a life of purpose no matter what your circumstances.

—Ruth Keidel Clemens

Family Tree

Only Those Mentioned in This Memoir

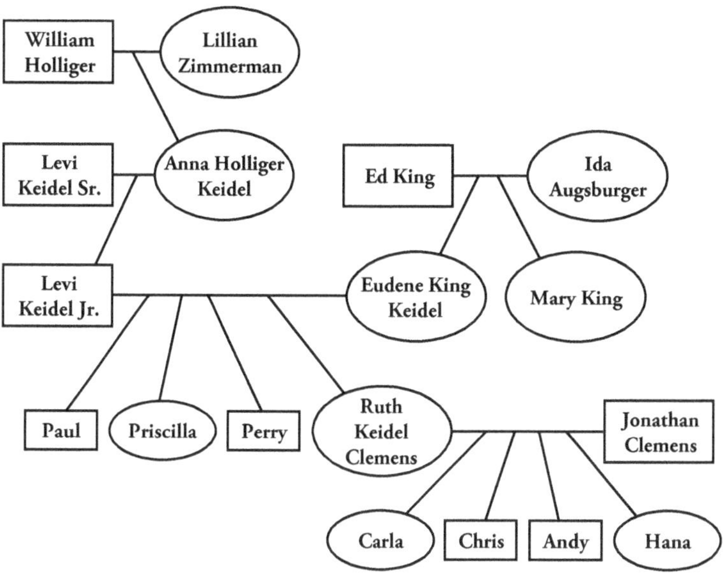

1

The Other Lakeshore

In a small cottage in the remote hills and forests of the Democratic Republic of Congo, Mom, Dad, and I were enjoying a vacation at Lake Madimape, which means "two lakes." There was the lake at the bottom of the steep hill below our cabin. Then there was what we called "the other lake" a mile away on the prairie.

In the evenings we sat on the front porch in the pitch dark. We watched the campfires that dotted the hillside across the lake. We listened to the gentle laughter and murmurings of the villagers. The stars were spread out like a huge net across the sky, the Milky Way so brilliant it seemed close enough to touch.

This lake had been my favorite vacation spot since I was a toddler. Retreating to this idyllic spot was one of the many benefits of growing up in Africa as a child of missionaries. I was home from boarding school for the summer after my junior year in high school. We were enjoying a much-anticipated break together in this isolated tropical paradise.

I was the youngest of four children, always trying to keep up with my older siblings. Now that they had all gone off to college in the United States, I enjoyed having my parents' attention to myself. The annual vacation pattern from boarding school was two weeks home at Christmas, two weeks home at Easter, and three months home in the summer.

High School Life in Kinshasa

During the school year while attending The American School of Kinshasa (TASOK), I lived in a hostel with other missionary kids. I played piano for the high school choir. I played basketball and soccer on the TASOK team against very competitive Congolese young women. The youth program at the International Protestant Church was active with Bible study every Monday evening. These times were key in my spiritual journey. On weekends we often went swimming in the Vampa Falls.

On Sunday evenings we frequently picnicked at the Stanley Monument where stood the statue of Sir Henry Morton Stanley with his arm stretched high over the vast expanse of the Congo River at Stanley Pool. Through his exploration of the Congo River in the late 1800s, Stanley opened the Congo Basin to the exploits of Belgian's King Leopold II. The statue was later torn down and replaced with the statue of an African warrior. The last time I saw the statue of Stanley, he was lying on his back in a warehouse, his arm outstretched toward the ceiling.

Statue of Morton Stanley

Just a couple months before this summer vacation, I had gotten involved with my first real boyfriend—a budding romance. He had gone to the United States for the summer to work at a camp in Wisconsin. We wrote letters to each other frequently that summer. He sent me poetry and photos he had taken and developed in his dark room. He was often on my mind as a gentle backdrop during those summer months.

Joy of Exploration

Back at Kalonda Station that summer, I enjoyed riding our small Honda 90 motorbike. Once in a while Dad sent me on errands. I especially enjoyed crossing the river to Tshikapa to get the third-class mail, magazines, and journals that had arrived on the slow boat from Kinshasa. I loved crossing the bridge, the loose cross-boards rattling beneath my motorcycle and the swift, brown Kasai River gliding past beneath me. Usually there were two large bags of mail to strap on the motorbike and take back across the river and up the hill to distribute to the missionaries at Kalonda.

During the day at Lake Madimape, I enjoyed the company of Chuck and Heidi Regier and their parents, Fremont and Sara, who were missionary colleagues vacationing in the cabin next door. Chuck and Heidi attended middle school at The American School of Kinshasa and lived with me in the Mennonite hostel. Chuck was always full of teasing and laughter. Heidi and I enjoyed playing piano together at the hostel.

Exploring the lakes, we discovered a small, sandy, gently sloping beach on the other side of the other lake. Not having swimsuits with us at that moment, we perched our hats on our hiking sticks, planted them firmly in the sand, and waded into the water. We pulled up our shorts so they wouldn't get wet. Of course, we soon got entirely soaked.

We hiked through fields of tall grass, stopping to take pictures of wild orchids. We walked through the tropical forest where the lush, green trees reached high above the jungle floor. Monkeys cackled at us from the branches. The cool dark green jungle smelled of damp earth.

We climbed up a hill to a big cliff overlooking the lake. We carved intricate detail on our hiking sticks with our pocketknives—our names, pictures of our favorite animals, and our lucky numbers.

We went with our families to picnic on the edge of the Monkey Ravine. We climbed down into the precipice, sinking into thick sand up to our knees. We did our best to avoid the wild monkeys that usually kept their distance on the cliffs above us.

Hunters from the local village walked past our cabin every evening, their small, barkless Basenji dogs in tow. They often had a recent catch of guinea fowl to sell. Women walked down the path behind our cabin on their way to and from their manioc fields. They carried large bowls of cassava on their heads, often with a baby tied to their backs and a small child in tow.

Church at Madimape

On Sundays we sat on low log benches in the little hut church in the village up the road where Pastor Poporo preached. This was a great way to practice our Tshiluba comprehension skills while watching small children play on the dirt floor.

Eudene playing her accordion in church

Dad took his turn preaching; he spoke Tshiluba better than most foreigners. Mom and her German accordion accompanied the old Western hymns translated into Tshiluba by Presbyterian missionaries generations ago.

But the best part about Congolese church was listening to their joyful traditional songs with intricate drumbeats on their goat skins stretched on hollowed logs. Children and women in red, blue, yellow, and green dresses danced joyfully in the aisles.

Gone Fishing

Mom spent much of her days fishing in a rowboat on the small lake at the bottom of the steep hill. She caught small tilapia and catfish to fry in peanut oil for every meal. Mom walked up the hill at the end of every morning, flushed from the sun and proud of her daily catch. She fried fish for lunch and supper and put the rest in the kerosene freezer for the next day.

Eudene goes fishing

Dad fished, too, but used a nightline that he set up with baited hooks every couple of feet. One end of the fishline was tied to an overhanging tree; the other end hung in the water overnight.

Brush with Death

Early one morning, Dad knocked on my bedroom door. "Get up, Ruth. Come and help me get the fish off my nightline." I quickly put on shorts and a T-shirt, and eagerly followed Dad out the cabin door. We took the bucket and inner tube and headed out the main road toward "the other lake," and we were off to our next adventure. Green and yellow grasshoppers flew ahead of our steps. The big red ball of a dry season sun was just peeking above the trees and vines of the dark green forest.

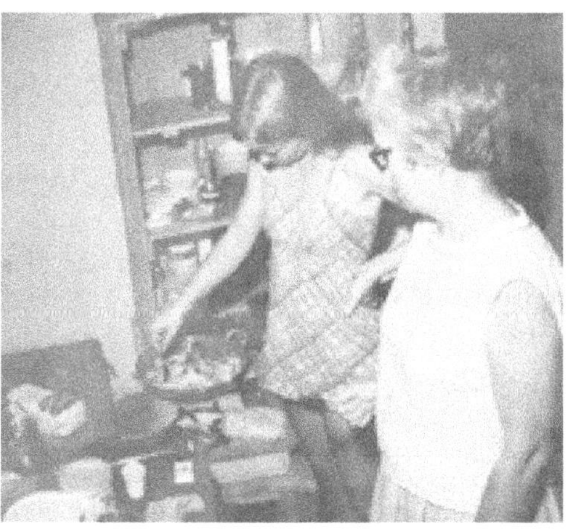

Ruth fries Mom's fish for dinner

A half mile down the road we turned right onto a well-worn footpath and rounded the water's edge. There we stopped at the foot of a tree extending out over the water where Dad had tied a nightline the evening before.

I eagerly climbed up the overhanging tree. I started hauling the line in while Dad got into the inner tube in the water below. He took the fish off the hooks one by one and plopped them into the bucket. We were overjoyed with our catch.

I had not noticed the large wasp nest just above me until I felt the sharp stings on my head, then on my arms, and then on my legs. The wasps kept coming. I shimmied off the tree as I yelled, "Dad, something is stinging me."

Dad quickly got out of the water, leaving the fish-filled bucket, inner tube, and his glasses on the shore of the lake. We rushed back up the path toward the main road. I was panicking, pulling stingers out of my head and arms as we went. Each sting was as painful as the last, and they wouldn't stop stinging. Wasps were caught in my long hair and burrowing under my T-shirt. As we hurried down the main road, my left arm started to swell, turning a strange pale white. Dad said, "That arm of yours doesn't look so good. We need to hurry home."

I burst into our cabin where Mom was frying fish for breakfast. "Mom, I've been stung by wasps!" Mom, greatly concerned, helped me to bed. I was afraid of what might happen next. Dad rushed next door to alert Fremont and Sara of the emergency. They gathered behind our cabin, talking frantically about what they should do to help me.

I got up to go to the bathroom next to my room and passed out, knocking over the bucket by the bathroom sink. The clamor alerted my parents who came rushing in to find me lying unconscious on the bathroom floor.

As Mom and Dad picked me up to carry me back to bed, I woke up and said, "I just had a terrible dream that I was stung by a bunch of wasps." As I watched their look of concern and alarm, I said, "Oh! It wasn't a dream. It really happened." They gently laid me back down on my bed.

The nearest medical dispensary was 35 miles away where there might be medication available. There was no doctor within 150 miles. We had no car and no motorcycle. Fortunately, Mom and Sara were nurses. Dad, Fremont, and Pastor Poporo knew how to pray and held vigil on the front porch.

As soon as the neighbors in the village heard the news, a Congolese man offered to ride his bicycle 35 miles to the dispensary at Ndjoka Punda. He hoped to get there in time for the two-way radio broadcast at noon to contact the doctor and alert the mission community. He left immediately with a written message, going as fast as his rickety bike could carry him.

Meanwhile in the bedroom, my face became so pale that Mom couldn't tell where my lips ended and my skin began. My pulse was imperceptible as Mom tried desperately to find it on both sides of my wrists. Mom was usually a calm person, but this was different. I could tell from her panic that things were not going well.

By that time, I had a clear sense that I might die that day. Yet in the midst of the terror and panic around me, I felt a tremendous sense of peace at the moment when I was closest to death. I thought to myself, "If this is how it feels to die, I'm ready. This really doesn't feel so bad."

Years later I read an account of someone who came near death after a poisonous snake bite. He described feeling a numb euphoria with no fear of death, which described my experience that day. Was I just feeling the euphoric effects of poison pulsing through my veins? Or was it the near presence of God that was comforting me?

Sara pulled out *The Merck Manual* for physicians, which instructed to force fluids into "both ends" to get the poison out of the digestive system and keep it from going into the blood stream. Mom cleaned out the siphoning hose used to fill the fridge with kerosene. The two innovative nurses used this hose to give me an enema.

Sara forced me to drink warm bitter tea, which I threw up and struggled to drink. I felt exhausted and tired of throwing up and refused the tea. Sara squatted down to my eye level and called me by my Congolese name. She said ever so gently but firmly, "Luta, you must drink this tea because we *want* you to throw up." With that encouragement, I complied.

My very weak, slow pulse lasted twenty minutes, but it seemed like hours. After three hours of forcing fluids, I finally stopped vomiting and fell asleep from exhaustion. This internal cleansing treatment with a kerosene siphoning hose is what saved my life.

When I woke up, Mother was standing on the side veranda looking past the trees to the sky above. She told me later that she was praying, "Lord, I love my daughter, but she is your child. If you want her more than I do, she is yours. But please give me the grace to bear whatever you ask of me."

Later that afternoon I awoke again to the sound of a motorcycle coming up the long lane. I peeked out my bedroom window to see a young American man astride a Honda 90. He handed some medicine to my mother and said, "Dr. Zook told me that by the time I got here, Ruth would either be better or wouldn't have made it. I'm so glad she's okay."

As I lay in bed listening to the conversation outside my window, I ran my fingers through my long hair, inspecting every inch of my scalp. I pulled several wasp heads out of my skull, digging deeply to be sure I got the stingers out along with the heads. The wasps were small but mighty. I also pulled stingers out of my arms and legs. I counted at least twenty bites. I wondered if anyone else had ever survived such an attack of killer wasps in Africa.

Miracle Survival

That evening in the cabin alone, Dad said, "You know, Ruth, it's a miracle you're alive. There's some reason why you were allowed to live today. God must have a purpose for your life."

That night, I had to wonder at the miracle of surviving this crisis and what it all meant for my life ahead. I was grateful that I would be able to go back to Kinshasa and enjoy my senior year of high school with close friends. I was glad I would see my boyfriend again. I was looking forward to playing the piano and dribbling a basketball down the court. I was looking forward to exploring colleges for the following year in the United States. I was so glad that I was given back my life to live with a promising future.

I thought about the local Congolese boy who had drowned just three weeks before when he tried to escape the wasps on the shore of "the other lake." Pastor Poporo said the boy jumped into the lake but couldn't swim well. Every time he came up for air, the swarm of wasps were there above the water waiting to attack him again.

Why hadn't God spared this boy's life? I could only imagine the deep grief his mother bore as she mourned the loss of her child. She likely heard about my experience that day and wondered how God had allowed me to survive and not her son.

All I really knew was a sense of tremendous relief and gratitude that in this remote part of Africa, I had survived this crisis.

I have often pondered Dad's words over the decades. This near-death experience made me grateful for the gift of each day and a desire to live life with purpose. This touchpoint of my life was a gentle reminder to make decisions that are worthy of a life that could have easily ended that day in an African paradise.

2

Journey Out of Congo

As our family lay on the blanket on our front veranda in Banga, gazing at the Southern Cross and the Milky Way, Dad said suddenly, "Hey, kids, you know we may have to leave Congo soon." (2.1)

Priscilla, Ruth, Perry and Paul Keidel 1959

"Why, Dad? When do we have to leave? When will we come back home to Banga?" Dad hesitated as we peppered him with questions, not knowing how to respond. As a four-year-old and the youngest of four children, I had no memory of any other home but Banga. I had been in Congo since I was eight months old.

I had already started to become aware that I was different than the many African children around me and was set apart as an American child of missionaries. When I was three years old, I stood with Mom outside the thatch-roofed church as children spilled out the door when church was over. As my African friends played tag on the church yard, I looked at my arm, and I looked at them. I turned to Mom and said, "Their skin is black, and my skin is pink, right?" "Yes, that's right," she said.

It was June 1960, and Congo was soon to gain independence from eighty years of Belgian colonial rule. The country's independence day was fast approaching. The Banga school needed a new flag to represent the new independent Republic of Congo. My mother, Eudene, was tasked with that sewing project.

Outside the mission stations, Americans, Canadians, and Europeans—whether these white foreigners were missionaries or colonial administrators—were not trusted in the eyes of the general Congolese population as they moved toward independence. By this time, my parents were becoming more aware that our family was at risk.

King Leopold's Invitation

During the late 1800s, King Leopold II of Belgium had enslaved the Congolese in their own country with forced labor to extract rubber and other natural resources, all to enrich his personal coffers (2.2). To control the Congolese laborers, the Belgian rulers cut off hands and used frequent whippings and other brutalities. In the early 1900s, King Leopold II turned Congo over to be ruled by a Belgian colonial authority who continued strict rule, taxation, and forced labor.

Eudene sews the Congo flag for Banga School

In the late 1800s (2.3), Leopold invited American, Canadian, and European missionaries—both Catholic and Protestant—to develop schools and hospitals. Many mission agencies saw this as an opportunity to improve the lives of the Congolese. This invitation was the beginning of missionary activity throughout Congo. During those years, there was no other way to operate in Congo outside of Belgian colonial structures.

Leaving Banga

Two weeks after the star-gazing evening, our family packed up what little we could carry to get ready to flee the possible chaos that was looming. Mom said, "Now, there won't be much room in the car. Just pack a couple sets of clothing and bring your suitcase out to the front porch to wait."

I gently set my doll and Teddy bear against my pillow and said, "Goodbye, Mary. Goodbye, Teddy. I'll just be gone for a couple weeks. Then I'll be back to sleep with you again in my own bed."

The cars were packed, and we stood out on the dirt road in front of our house ready to pile in. Our Congolese friends and colleagues surrounded us, ready to say goodbye.

Levi points out Banga at the other end of the ravine

But Dad suddenly hesitated. He turned to Glenn Rocke, another missionary who had lived at Banga for many years, and said, “We can’t just pull out and abandon our Congolese friends like this, can we? We don’t know what kind of dangers they might confront with this transition.” Then Dad came up with an idea. “Why don’t we hide together in the deep ravine if the soldiers come and start looking for us? The thick jungle and vast expanse of the forest will hide us. Eudene, you go ahead with the children. We’ll stay here at the station to be with our colleagues and see what unfolds.”

I stared at Dad, not quite comprehending that he could think of sending us off on our own. I looked at Mom, the bright noon sun reflecting off her glasses. Her face was stoic as she took in this sudden new plan.

Glenn quickly agreed. “Good idea, Levi, let’s stay here and see what happens.”

I watched Mom slowly turn to get into the car. She said, “Come on kids, let’s go.”

As we drove away, I hopped onto my knees and turned around to look out the back window and watch Dad and Glenn. Surrounded by a small crowd, they gradually disappeared in a cloud of dry-season dust. I wondered when I would see Dad again. Mom sat in the front seat stone-faced, staring straight ahead, a tear streaming down her cheek.

Later we learned that after we left, Pastor Kituba turned to Dad and Glenn, and kindly explained, “Preachers, you don’t know enough about living off leaves and berries in the forest to survive. It might be difficult for us to protect you from soldiers who will likely come through Banga looking for you. We'll have to feed you, and they'd find out where you are." Other bystanders leaned in, listening closely. They all nodded in agreement and said, "*Eyo*! Yes, this is true! You must leave us even for our own safety."

So finally, Dad and Glenn bade them farewell and proceeded to follow the caravan out of Banga.

Anxious Deliberation

By that night, about ten missionary families had all relocated southwest to Kandala to determine their next move. Children were put to bed in one large room while parents gathered in a big circle in the living room to deliberate.

I lay in bed looking at the row of mosquito nets across the dimly lit bedroom. Their shadows moved on the walls as a light breeze came through the open windows. I imagined that the other children were sleeping soundly. I could hear adults discussing in hushed urgent tones in the living room.

"I think we need to leave Congo altogether."

"Really? But where will we go?"

"South to Angola."

"But who do we know there? Where would we stay with all our children?"

"There are Methodist missionaries down there. They'll help us out."

I started to cry and called my mother. I wanted her to comfort me and tell me that everything would be okay—that this was just a short trip like going to the lake for vacation, that we would go home soon. But maybe my mother didn't hear me. Maybe she was caught up in the discussion and didn't want to miss out on anything.

Soon Gladys Graber, my best friend's mother, came into the bedroom and picked me up from under the mosquito net. She sat down with me in the rocking chair at the foot of the bed. She held me tightly, sang, and rocked me. Feeling the comfort of her close embrace, I finally fell asleep.

By the next afternoon it became clear that all the missionary families needed to relocate across the southern border to Angola for safety. Having brought along no food, the men loaded barrels of preserves from Jim and Jenny Bertsche's attic into a big truck while Jenny supervised. As a missionary family planning to live in Congo for four years, they had stored barrels of provisions to last for another couple of years. Their daughter came upstairs, only to see the young men clearing out their attic. She cried, "Mother, are they going to take all our canned food and Christmas presents too?"

Soon Jenny's husband Jim came trudging up the steps and said, "Jenny, I think we should stay to support our Congolese colleagues through this turmoil, don't you?"

Jenny stood in the middle of the attic floor, comforting her daughter who was afraid of losing everything, and pondered her husband's request to stay through the turmoil with their Congolese colleagues.

Jenny decided that day that she was going to put her children's safety first. Jim agreed to leave with the rest of the missionaries, but later in life he still struggled with regrets about this decision, as did many others.

Driving Out of Congo

That afternoon a long caravan of missionaries drove south to Angola, continuing through the night. I watched out my back window as cars with Belgian colonial authorities zoomed past us in quick retreat, fleeing the violence and turmoil behind them. We went through villages where stones were in the road—thrown at vehicles that had gone ahead of us. From the back seat, I could see the tension in Dad's face, the veins rising in his neck. I knew then that this wasn't just a fun traveling adventure.

Crossing the Angolan border

At daybreak, after crossing the Angolan border, we came to a stream where the other missionaries were waiting for us. We were the last of the missionary caravan to retreat out of

Congo. We took baths in the cold stream, washed our dusty clothes, and boiled water on a campfire for tea to quench our thirst on that dry-season ride.

Bathing south of the Congo/Angola border

Then the missionary caravan of twenty vehicles drove all day through Northern Angola. I watched this desolate and quiet land go by—tall, dry, brown grass on either side; baobab trees in the distance; a lone cow herder every so often.

Caravan through northern Angola

We traveled farther and farther from the security of home. Brother Perry became sick and lay on the floor of the VW Combi as the dry season dust floated up through the floorboards.

Contacting U.S. headquarters by ham radio from northern Angola (Ruth on the left)

We found a convenient place to stop along the isolated road. Someone got their ham radio out and contacted the mission board in the United States to let them know that everyone was safely evacuated out of Congo.

Catholic Priests Welcome Missionaries and Colonial Administrators

Continuing on our journey through Angola, we saw in the distance a tall, white church steeple of a welcoming Catholic mission. We all felt a sense of relief to find this oasis in northern Angola. By this time, several Belgians had joined us. Whether American missionary or Belgian colonialist, everyone felt the grief and loss of having to suddenly leave Congo, uncertain when we would be allowed to return.

That night the women and children slept in the priests' bedroom—six large beds in one large room. After the lights were out and everyone was settled, a missionary lady from across the room said, "This is the first time I've slept in a priest's bed." Polite laughter rippled across the room. A missionary lady from the other side of the room said, "Well, it's a good thing you're not sleeping with the priest." Loud laughter followed. We never found out where the priests slept that night.

Catholic parish in northern Angola

The men and older boys slept outside in the cars. During the night, the lions started roaring in the grassy prairie nearby.

I could hear them from where I was sleeping by Mom's feet at the bottom of the bed. I wondered if my brothers were safe in the car outside.

On their way into the parish, Dad had to relieve himself. Paul held the lantern for him, trembling while the lions' roars came closer. I was finally able to sleep once I heard the men come through the parish door.

Decision Point in Angola

The next morning we made our way to Quessua, a Methodist mission school farther south. Fortunately, the students were gone for the summer holiday. Sheets were hastily hung up in classrooms for privacy. I fell asleep listening to the low murmurs of private family conversations across thin dividers.

Arrival at Quessua, Methodist mission in Angola

Our hope was to stay in Angola for a week or two and go back to Congo when things had calmed down. However, the Portuguese colonial authorities became nervous. The

Angolans, hearing what was going on in Congo, were catching on to the idea of independence as well. They might revolt against their colonial rulers. So the missionaries were asked to leave Africa.

Jim Bertsche (center) delivering word that they must leave Africa. (Levi on right holding camera)

It was at this point that the missionaries finally realized, with deep regret, that they would be away from their homes in Congo for more than the assumed two weeks.

Boarding the train at Malanga, Angola

The caravan of missionaries then drove to Malanga, the trailhead. They abandoned their cars and took the train to Loanda, the capital city on the west coast of Angola.

Flying Home

In Loanda, we boarded several military transport planes that had dropped off UN forces who were activated to restore order in Congo. Once inside the aircraft, Dad laid out his scratchy wool blanket on the floor of the plane for me to lie on. The interior of the plane was cavernous and dark. There were only rope seats along the sides for a few to sit on. Having no interest in sleep, I crawled around on the hard, canvassed floor between missionaries and Belgians. They were all cramped together, hugging their knees to their chests. Many were staring vacantly into space as I disturbed their thoughts with my restlessness. I was excited to be on my first airplane ride.

Settling in for the long flight out of Angola

I watched jealously as a UN trooper lifted my brother Perry onto his shoulders, stepped carefully through the crowd, and entered the cockpit. Perry came back bragging about sitting on the pilot's lap and "driving" the plane. I asked Mom why I couldn't go into the cockpit as well. "Oh, that's just for the boys," she said. I was deeply disappointed.

For several days we traveled north across Africa through Ghana, Tunisia, and on to France. Then we finally flew to New York City. Media reporters milled around JFK Airport, eager to talk with these refugees fresh from the turmoil in Congo. It was all over international news. My mother felt exhausted. In a faded, wrinkled, mid-calf dress with four hungry children following her through the airport, she waved off the journalists as best she could.

Missionaries and Colonialism

I wonder about the work of the missionaries during colonial times. They established medical and educational systems, mentoring peace-loving Congolese leadership. Yet these hospitals and schools had to be part of the colonial infrastructure to exist in Congo.

My father started elementary schools in the Banga area, providing their first formal education. My mother started medical dispensaries where there had never been a formal health care system before.

Belgium's King Leopold II plundered Congo through genocidal means. He decreased its population by approximately ten million through his brutalizing practices in the late 1800s. (2.2)

Some of the earlier missionaries who went to Congo at the turn of the century confronted internal slavery and abusive practices in the rubber fields. They heard about the whippings and cutting off of hands for punishment. Some missionaries became instrumental in raising international awareness of these abuses taking place in the Kasai Rubber Company specifically. (2.3) Through their protests and witness, the governance of Congo changed from King Leopold's personal property to a Belgian colonial authority with less brutality, even though Congo continued to be a Belgian colony.

Between 1947 and 1960, missionary teachers went through Brussels on their way to Congo to take French language studies. They were also obligated to take the Belgian Colonial Course—Belgian history, Belgian system of law, Belgian colonial philosophy, and state/church relations in Congo. Taking this course was a prerequisite to receive colonial subsidies for mission work in Congo. These subsidies helped expand the missions' education and health work. Receiving these subsidies while increasing the reach of their work presented a great dilemma for many missionaries who knew the subsidies had been raised through taxation of the Congolese. (2.4)

I knew the missionaries, including my parents, had a desire to enhance the lives of the Congolese people. I also knew they could only do their work in Congo under the colonial infrastructure. I continue to hold these dilemmas uneasily.

Living with the Guilt of Abandonment

The evacuation of missionaries from Congo in 1960 strained the relationship between missionaries and Congolese church leaders. The leaders felt abandoned in many cases, even though they had advised the missionaries to leave. At the same time, this "abandonment" became an opportunity for the Congolese church to become more independent and self-sustaining.

Many missionaries lived on with a sense of guilt from that experience. Most were determined not to repeat this scenario in years to come, no matter what the consequences. This resolve was severely tested just four years later.

3

Praying Us Out of the Rebellion

It was 1964 at the height of the Kwilu Rebellion in Western Congo. This was a revolutionary and military response to what some Congolese felt were unfair social and economic practices by their government following independence in 1960.

Swedish UN Peacekeepers, Mr. Neilsen and Mr. Steinberg, with Eudene, Perry, Ruth and Jeanette

The United Nations assigned two Swedish peacekeepers to accompany my dad on his trips with the bookmobile. He continued to set up bookstores and distribute

Christian literature throughout the Kasai Provinces despite rebel activity in those regions.

Trauma of the Congolese

One afternoon I watched from the kitchen window as a large truck of Congolese men, women, and children rumbled onto our backyard to find shelter from the violence in their villages. After they had been camping out in our yard for several days, I peered into the back of the truck. I noticed an elderly woman perched inside under the canopy with a haunting and fearful look in her eyes. I wondered what trauma she had experienced when she had to leave her home behind.

When I was eight years old, Misenga became my neighbor in Kananga when her adoptive British parents moved in next door. Her birth family had been attacked by the rebels, and her parents had been killed. Misenga's right arm was cut off during this machete attack.

Playing with ten-year-old Misenga in her backyard, I watched her use her left arm adeptly to start a fire. Then she cracked an egg into the frying pan and scrambled it as it fried. We shared breakfast together by the sandbox.

An Orphan Boy

That same year, Bidwai came to live in the open alcove under the eaves near Dad's bookstore. He was an orphan left to wander the streets of Kananga during the war and the starvation of this time. He was eight years old, like me. This thin, slight boy found his way to our back door one day, begging for food. He asked if we could help him find a place to stay.

Dad's bookstore colleagues talked with Bidwai for a long time. They determined that he was truly an orphan who needed help. At that time there were no services available in Kananga for orphaned children. The numbers of these children rose as the rebellion raged in the country. So Dad set up a cot in the open alcove and gave him a blanket and a pillow.

"Mom," I asked, "why can't Bidwai live in our house with us or even come into the house and play?"

"Oh, he'll see all the things we have and learn what he's missing out on. He might steal your toys."

Mom gave the boy some of my brother Perry's shirts, shorts, and underwear. Mom often reminded Bidwai to tuck his shirt into his pants, not into his underwear.

One day I peered into his outdoor shelter. I wondered if he truly felt safe among the spiders and rats that accompanied him in that dark, damp space. Well, I thought, at least he's not living on the streets.

Bidwai lived in that alcove for several months. But one day he left without a word, and we never heard from him again. I hoped he had found a better place to live. I was sad that he would never know the love and care of a parent who would provide a clean bed and a cool bath when he got malaria.

Maybe Bidwai decided he was better off on his own

than being subject to my father's somewhat harsh discipline. I knew Dad was trying to help Bidwai become a well-behaved boy who could function in society, but I had to wonder how successful Dad was in truly helping him.

Finding Refuge in Our Home

Soon after Bidwai left, the news came that the Graber and Bertsche families had been burned out of their homes in Kandala by the rebels. (3.1) The missionary families in Kananga poured out their sympathy by collecting toys for their children, Jeanette and Tim. I saw the luxurious stack of dolls and toy trucks piled up in someone's dining room and designated for my friends. I secretly wished my house would burn down so I could get so many nice new toys.

Jeannette, Basenji and Ruth

After this crisis, these two families came to Kananga to rest. Uprooted, they were not sure how to plan their next move. Many afternoons I watched as Jeannette's mother, whom I called Aunt Gladys, paced the living room floor—back and forth, back and forth—pondering what they had just been through as a family.

Jeanette slept with me in my double bed. It was like having a slumber party every night. She spent many hours after lights out telling me how she held onto her daddy's neck while the rebels circled around her family, threatening to kill them while a circle of fire was gradually encroaching. She had watched as the rebels yanked the curlers out of her mother's hair, claiming they were antennae to communicate with the government. She talked of living in the school building with her parents for three days, barefoot in her pajamas, waiting to be rescued by a helicopter. I went to sleep holding her fear in my heart while I absorbed her stories.

The Long Prayer Meeting

As the rebels advanced closer to our city of Kananga, the Mennonite and Presbyterian missionaries held a prayer meeting to determine whether they should stay or leave Congo. This decision weighed heavily on their hearts, recalling how they had abandoned the Congolese church just four years earlier in 1960. They didn't want to do the same again so soon.

I was with the other missionary children in a large classroom, singing songs, playing games, and coloring pictures while our parents deliberated in the large auditorium across the courtyard. It seemed the service was taking very long, and

I was getting tired and impatient. I was ready to go home and go to bed.

I slipped out of the classroom and walked through the courtyard of the retreat center. The pungent smell of white and yellow Franji Panni petals wafted through the cool evening air.

I peered inside the door of the large auditorium, ceiling fans whirring above. There I saw Dad and Mom standing with the congregation who were all holding the bread and cup of communion. They were slowly and somberly singing, "Oh, Jesus I have promised to serve Thee to the end."

I knew then and there that we weren't going home very soon. And there was no way we were going to leave Congo this time, even if the rebels came to town.

Later that night when we finally got home, I asked Dad if everything was going to be okay. He tried to reassure me. But I could tell by the lines on his forehead and the bags under his eyes that he was very worried. It seemed inevitable that the rebels would take our city of Kananga.

The next morning, I said a tearful goodbye to Jeanette, my first best friend. Dad took her family to the airport to fly back to the United States to save them from yet more turmoil.

On the way to the airport, they saw many military trucks packed with heavily armed national Congolese military soldiers. Foxholes had been dug in the tall grassy fields surrounding the airport. Soldiers were embedded in foxholes with camouflage branches on their helmets.

Ruth and Jeannette by the Kasai River

That night we didn't sleep well. Dad laid his clothes out next to his bed in case he had to dress quickly in the middle of the night. He lay awake waiting for the sound of battle.

However, the next morning, word came that the rebels had been defeated in a brutal battle with the Congolese military right outside our city. The rebels were no longer a threat to Kananga or to the rest of the country.

We felt a tremendous sense of relief. But as a young child, I had to wonder. Was this an answer to the prayers of the missionaries and Congolese Christians?

"God," I prayed, "why didn't you stop the rebels earlier? Why did Jeanette and Tim have to suffer the trauma of watching their homes go up in flames? Why did they have to live in their pajamas until they were rescued by a helicopter three days later? Why didn't you save all the other thousands of lives that have been lost along the way?"

Where Did Their Resiliency Come From?

What was it about my parents' background that gave them such a sense of purpose, resiliency, and determination to help others that they would put their family at risk during war and uncertainty? What events in their earlier lives gave them each a sense of determination to serve abroad and raise a family in Congo during such tumultuous times?

4

Developing Resiliency and Determination

A sudden, terrible flood or accident might have been more bearable to the Holliger family. But as it was, the disease came silently and stealthily, and took the children one by one. For several days in a row, Mr. Foster, the undertaker, came up the hill to the Holliger farmhouse with his lazy, brown horses and spring wagon to take the bodies away. (4.1)

My paternal grandmother, Anna Holliger, was nineteen at the time. She watched closely from her upstairs bedroom window. Mr. Foster took a tiny glass bottle out of his pocket and carefully placed a small pink pill onto his tongue, as Dr. Miller had instructed. This was supposed to keep him from catching the deadly disease. Anna's mother, Lillian, was once again out on the front porch with her dead child's body, waiting for Mr. Foster to take yet another one away.

It was 1918 when the global flu pandemic, known as

the Spanish flu, hit the United States and the Holliger farm in Central Illinois. By 1920, this deadly disease would kill about fifty million people worldwide.

The Holliger family became sick one by one, Anna's father falling ill first. The family slept downstairs on the couch and make-shift beds so Lillian could care for all of them in one room. Anna watched as her father paced restlessly from one end of the house to the other. He carefully stepped through the maze of children, blankets, and pillows laying askew throughout the living room. Beads of sweat lined his worried forehead.

"Mother," he said, touching her shoulder, "if I could only scrub my stomach out with a scrub brush, I'm sure I'd feel better." He soon went into a coma and died in the living room. Mr. Foster came to carry his body away.

Lillian called the influenza specialist from Peoria and said, "I have a houseful of sick children. Please come and examine everyone so I know how to care for them." The specialist came and examined each child.

"Mrs. Holliger," he said, "There's a good chance your whole family will die except for Anna who seems like an especially sturdy young woman." With this assessment, he charged Lillian $100 and went back to Peoria. The family then went into home quarantine. Lillian bathed every child daily, rubbing each of their bodies with olive oil to comfort them.

The day after their father's death, five-year-old Raymond and twelve-year-old Elizabeth also died. All three were buried in the same grave on the hill behind the church. Within a few days, their sister Katherine and brother Arthur died as well. Lillian held her feelings at bay, having little time to grieve the loss of each child and becoming numb in mind and body.

Anna shared the double bed upstairs with her sister Emma. Their fevers broke at the same time after being ill together for a month. Anna continued to improve, but Emma became feverish again. Anna watched as Emma struggled to breathe in the bed next to her.

Anna Hollinger Keidel

"Mother," she called, "I'm afraid Emma's not going to make it through the night." By the time Mother came upstairs, Emma was gone. They gently closed her hazel eyes, and Mother once again called Mr. Foster to take Emma's still body away.

In the span of one month, Anna had lost her father and five siblings. When her fever broke, she carefully swung her legs over the edge of the bed. It was painful to stand up since she hadn't walked for a few weeks except to go to the bathroom. She put the pillow on the floor beneath her feet, easing the pain as she gingerly stood up.

Anna walked slowly to the top of the stairs and looked down into the living room. The house was so quiet—no running and laughing children. Anna wept, grieving her sudden losses. Only Anna, her mother, her two younger sisters who had stayed with their Aunt Ruth, and her brother who had come home from the military were left to carry on. Their grief was especially acute when they sat down at the long, wooden dining room table for dinner with six empty chairs.

The dead had been buried behind the Christian Apostolic church up on the hill. The yellow daffodils by the front porch were beginning to peek up out of the ground.

Anna helped her mother wash all the bedding and hang it out on the clothesline to dry in the backyard. She hung up the pillows that had comforted her brothers and sisters. She hung up Lillian's handmade, finely stitched quilts with floral patterns of red, green, blue, and yellow, and watched them flap in the cool, spring breeze.

Levi's Journey

Some years later, Anna married and bore a child, Levi, my father. He fell critically ill at two months old. The doctor gave baby Levi three days to live. Desperately, Anna fell to her knees next to the bed where the child lay in the hospital. She gently pinched the skin on his tiny arm to see the "tent" form. She knew that this demonstrated severe dehydration. "Dear God," she prayed, "Please spare this precious child, and I will allow you to do with him as you wish." (4.2)

Years later, Levi, then a young adult just returned from the Navy, said to his mother over the dinner table, "How would you feel if I wanted to become a missionary?" At first, Anna was shocked at the thought. My son, a missionary?

Having been distant from the church for many years, this was an unusual concept for her.

Anna soon recalled the prayer she had offered twenty-one years before and said, “Well, if you think that’s what God wants you to do, then you’d better do it.”

Anna Holliger Keidel’s resilience and determination was characteristic of her life. These qualities became part of Levi’s approach to life as well as he pursued an unusual calling.

Levi’s father—also named Levi—was a tenant farmer. He moved from one farm to another with a growing family as they struggling through the Great Depression to make ends meet. The younger Levi acutely felt the insecurity in his family. But because Levi showed promise in school, Anna raised chickens and sold the eggs to pay for a tutor so he could advance in his reading and writing skills.

Levi was a very curious and rambunctious boy and teenager with little discipline. As a young man of seventeen, he began to yearn for a more productive and focused life. At one point he prayed, “God, if I ever learn what to do to get right with you, I’ll do my best for the rest of my life to show you I appreciate it.”

Although he was the salutatorian of his high school class, Levi had to piece together his college education. His family couldn’t afford to send him for further education.

Levi was able to pull together his college degree because of his determination. Ten years later he received a master’s in journalism, and many years later, he earned a master’s in missions and evangelism.

At nineteen, Levi enlisted in the Navy. It was toward the end of World War II. He served as a radio transmitter engineer. This training would later allow him to set up the radio communication system for Mennonite mission stations in Congo. While he was serving in the Navy, a friend guided him toward a commitment to God.

When Levi was discharged from the military in 1946, he knew he had to seek out a new set of friends back home in Illinois. He was in touch with an old girlfriend who introduced him to Eudene, a nursing school friend. Meeting Eudene, who was determined to be a missionary in Africa, set him on the focused path he was looking for.

Levi had a strong determination to make a significant impact on the church in Congo. In the 1950s he started elementary schools in a remote part of Congo among the Bashele people, who had never had a traditional education.

Levi hands out literature from the book-mobile

In the early 1960s, Levi set up a literature distribution system for Mennonite and Presbyterian missions in the Kasai regions. He wrote Christian literature in Tshiluba. He set up local bookstores and trained the managers of these stores. This Christian literature distribution system became a model for other mission groups throughout Africa. Later, Levi and Eudene organized conferences throughout the Kasai region, mentoring pastors in church leadership.

My father taught me that God has a purpose for my life. He encouraged me from a young age to pursue a sense of meaning in daily life. Largely because of my dad's influence, I, too, developed a desire to pursue life with purpose.

5

Where's Mom?

When Eudene was nine years old, she responded to the nudging of God's Spirit to be a missionary in Congo after hearing a returned missionary speak at Flanagan Mennonite Church. From that day on, she was determined to become a missionary nurse.

Eudene, John Zook, Agnes Sprunger
with medical colleagues at Banga Dispensary

In the late 1800s to early 1900s, amid the cornfields in Central Illinois, several Mennonite communities began to reach out beyond themselves. These committed Mennonites created Meadows Retirement Community, Mennonite Hospital of Bloomington, and City Home Mission in Chicago. (5.1)

In 1912, this same group began sending mission workers to the Belgian Congo through Congo Inland Mission. Some of these early missionaries died of malaria and sleeping sickness, but others continued their work in Congo. Those who returned spoke in churches throughout central Illinois to raise support and inspire young people to join the effort. Amidst the surge of post-World War II missionaries were Eudene and Levi Keidel.

Eudene and Paul weighing babies at Banga

Throughout the 1950s, the predominant image of women in the United States was stay-at-home housewives who kept the house sparkling clean and cooked three hardy meals a day. However, Eudene had a different calling.

From 1951 through 1956, Eudene gave birth to four children and cared for them—and I was the youngest. At the same time, from 1952 to 1960, she established several medical dispensaries for the Bashele people in Congo. In the isolation of rural mission stations, Eudene made medical decisions that physicians usually made. Over thirty-three years of mission work, she delivered hundreds of babies and also trained midwives. She taught primary health care to new mothers and medical skills to Congolese nurses.

Loss of a Big Sister

When Eudene was ten years old, her older sister, Mary, died of bulbar polio. In 1931, this type of polio swept through Livingston County, Illinois. These children died slowly of suffocation. Fourteen-year-old Mary was the fifth child to die of this disease in the small farming community of Flanagan, Illinois.

Ida and Ed King (back) with Eudene (front left) and Mary (front right)

Neighbors would not enter the house for fear of catching the disease, so the house was fumigated. Mary's body was displayed in the big bay window in the living room at the old white farmhouse. A small funeral was held in the yard. Eudene and her parents spent that night in quarantine in the big red barn behind the house.

Eudene deeply missed Mary and wondered why God had taken her. A kind neighbor gave Eudene a beautiful China doll for comfort. That doll rested on her pillowed bed wherever Eudene lived throughout her life.

This is what I imagine from my mother's stories of that loss in her life:

Mary lies in her mother's big brass bed

Doctor, Father, Mother watch

And wait

The last shot eases the inevitable suffocation by polio.

Ten-year-old Eudene peers from the living room through the bedroom door,

Her view blocked by adults who don't want her to see Mary suffer.

Eudene runs around through the kitchen, pantry, bathroom of the big farmhouse

To the other bedroom door

Hoping for one last glimpse of her sister

Alive.

She hears Mary's soft last words,

"Goodbye, Eudene."

The family sleeps in the barn that night,

Afraid of polio infection that has ripped through the county.

Lonely, dark night

Lying on prickly hay

Racoons scuttling in high corners of the loft.

Eudene clutches a new China doll in a white dress with pink flowers

She received that day from a compassionate neighbor

For a small bit of comfort through that long night.

Determined to Go to Africa

While in nursing school, twenty-seven-year-old Eudene was set up for a blind date with Levi, who was six years her junior. On their first date, she told him she was going to Africa as a missionary. If he wasn't interested in such a life, they may as well drop the relationship right then and there.

Levi was a new Christian at the time. The idea of going to Africa sounded like a great adventure. It didn't take him long to get onboard with the plan.

Even though Levi's career would largely determine where the family lived from one term to the next, it was Eudene's quiet determination to follow her calling from a very young age that was the driving force behind their decision to go to Congo in 1952.

Eudene's Calling

As a young child, I became accustomed to Mom's work outside the home providing health care in the community. I recall as a three-year-old suddenly missing her and crying, "Mom, Mom, where's Mom?" We were living at Banga Station in the Kasai region of Congo, Central Africa. Kadima, our helper, took me out the front door and off the porch to our front lane. He bent way over to look me in the eyes. He pointed in the distance to the medical clinic about 100 yards away.

Eudene takes Ruth for a ride

There was Mom waving at me and smiling. As a nurse, she was busy seeing patients lined up outside the clinic. She must have heard me cry from the distance. I immediately calmed down and went back into the house to play, understanding that Mom would be home after clinic hours.

I loved riding in the large basket attached to the front of Mom's bike, and she didn't seem to think there was any danger of my falling out.

Each time we went back to Congo after a two-year furlough, Eudene prepared with great joy, enthusiasm, and sense of adventure. She always had a particular plan to use her gifts for the coming four-year term in Congo. Throughout her career, Eudene was involved in medical ministry and Bible teaching from five different stations in Congo.

Eudene's public health training chart

Eudene taught me and many other missionary children how to play the piano. We were fortunate to have the only real piano among the Mennonite and Presbyterian missionaries in Congo. This shiny, black console was given to us by a colonial administrator who had to flee Congo in 1960. Many evenings Mom accompanied Dad on the violin as we dozed off to sleep. Most afternoons my mom played classical music on the record player. This constant musical exposure formed the roots of my love for classical music.

A Clear Sense of Purpose

Mom had a clear sense of God's purpose for her life and was a quiet influence on many. Growing up in this environment gave me a desire to be part of something bigger than myself. I came to understand that we all have a place in God's mission in the world, wherever we are, in whatever we do, and relating to all aspects of life.

6

A Nine-Year-Old Leaves Home

I turned ten at Central School, the Presbyterian boarding school in Lubondai. February 9, 1966, Aunt Martha came to English class to pull me out. She took me to the school kitchen. At first, I thought I was in trouble.

As a missionary community, the children addressed all missionary colleagues and teachers as "Aunt" and "Uncle" as though we were part of one big family. Aunt Martha showed me the cake the cooks had made for my birthday. She asked if it looked like what I had requested. I looked at the golden, shiny, brown icing on the three-decker cake displayed on the high counter. Tatu Mputa, the cook, looked gently at me and smiled.

"Yes! That looks very nice," I exclaimed, nodding vigorously. Then she sent me back to Aunt Phyllis's English class.

Our birthday treat at Central School was to choose the kind of cake we wanted for our special day. I knew I wanted a caramel cake. I had never had one before, but it sounded really good.

Laughing Sarah

My favorite class at Central School was Bible class. That's where I first remember equating the story of Abraham leaving his country with our missionary parents leaving their American homes for Africa in response to God's call.

When we memorized the books of the Bible, my classmate Jeff illustrated how the last book of the Old Testament, Malachi, sounds like the Southern Presbyterian pronunciation of the Tshiluba word for "How are you?" We'd get to the last book in our recitation, and he'd say "*Malu kai?*" very loudly with a Southern drawl.

Aunt Peggy's music class, Ruth on the far left

Our Bible teacher, Aunt Peggy, loved to make the stories come alive through drama. She decided we should put on a play of Abraham and Sarah. I played Sarah. Steve, who I had a crush on at the time, played Abraham.

The most difficult scene for me was when an aged Sarah had to laugh in response to the angels telling Abraham she would get pregnant with a son. The best I could do was "ha-ha-ha." Aunt Peggy made me practice a "natural laugh" repeatedly one day until I got it down pat.

The big day was the performance for school chapel. At the right time, I stood behind the curtain and let out a "natural" laugh. I felt like I had conquered the world.

Scary Movie Night

My parents didn't allow us to watch movies when we were young. Maybe that was a good thing.

On Saturday evenings the Presbyterian school showed reel-to-reel movies every few weeks. We gathered in the large living room between the library and the boys' dormitory. *Annie Get Your Gun* was the first movie I ever saw.

But the most traumatic movie featured a dead, elderly, overweight, wealthy, white guy whose wife pushed him through an airport in a wheelchair, his big, dark sunglasses on. The most memorable scene was a close-up of his face when the dark sunglasses fell off his nose and his wide-open dead eyes filled the screen.

The other little girls were equally traumatized. That night

we gathered in the hallway back in our dorm, swapping scary stories. The idea that most captured our imagination was the likelihood that Hitler was still alive. He could have escaped to Africa. In fact, he might be hiding in the jungle right outside our boarding school.

Martha suggested we play "Hitler" after lights out. She played the lead role, hiding in one of the bedroom closets while we closed our eyes. Then we held hands and walked in and out of each bedroom, waiting for her to jump out and capture us.

Dictionary Detention

The mode of punishment in those days at Central School was to copy pages out of the *Oxford Dictionary*. Perhaps they thought it would teach us new vocabulary. What they didn't consider was its effect on the handwriting of children often subjected to this practice. This form of punishment also didn't help get energy out of the system on a Saturday morning.

"Playing Hitler" turned into a frequent pastime after lights out. Finally, Aunt Sarah, our dorm mother, caught us in the act. She ordered the whole dorm to spend a Saturday morning in dictionary detention.

Since my roommate Kathy and I were the youngest fourth graders, some of the older girls thought we should be exempt this time. Yet I knew I was guilty of being up after lights out and deserved the punishment. As it turned out,

Martha and the older girls were assigned a half page to copy; Kathy and I got only a quarter page.

That Saturday we dutifully copied words and definitions in the dark classroom, listening to the laughter of the other children playing outside on that bright sunny morning.

Alone with Malaria

It was common for me to get malaria as a child. The weekly Sunday morning dose of Daraprim was not as effective as it should have been. I recognized the symptoms quickly—achy fever and chills, loss of energy, and an overwhelming desire to lie down and watch the world go by.

As a trained nurse, Mom had a special touch to gently care for us when we were sick. When I threw up in the toilet, she held my forehead with a cool washcloth. She fixed chicken noodle soup for my queasy stomach and brought books for me to read. When we were in the United States, she allowed me to watch sitcoms all day—an unusual treat.

I distinctly recall the absence of her nursing attention when I was six years old and Mom, brother Perry, and I came down with malaria at the same time. One evening my temperature spiked to 106 degrees Fahrenheit. Dad bathed me in a cool tub to bring my temperature down while Mom lay helplessly in bed.

Being sick at boarding school was no fun without Mom. I lay in bed alone in the dorm, sleeping some of the time, staring at the ceiling most of the time. I marveled at the quiet inside the dorm and the loud chatter of my friends playing outside after school. Aunt Sarah came in occasionally to check on me and take my temperature.

This was the "sick rule" at Central School: Once your temperature is normal, you must get up and go back to class—no lazing around. After the third day of fever, my temperature broke. I still felt sick and weak, but according to the rule, I had to get up for breakfast and classes.

For some reason, I sat at the teachers' breakfast table that morning. Maybe they wanted to monitor me a bit. I lay my head down on the table to get a bit of rest between spoonsful of oatmeal. Uncle Sid asked, "Ruth, are you feeling okay?"

"No, I still feel pretty sick," I told him.

"Do you have a temperature?"

"No."

"Hmm, well then I guess you need to go to class."

I looked up at Aunt Phyllis who was sitting across the table and had a compassionate glint in her eyes. I wondered what she thought but wasn't allowed to ask.

So I went back to class like an obedient little missionary kid.

Six Cavities

The missionary dentist made his annual visit to Lubondai where he spent several weeks catching up on the dental needs of missionary kids at Central School. The Keidel kids were some of his most faithful customers.

I didn't take good care of my teeth at boarding school in the fourth grade. Somehow, I had missed that lesson at home. Perhaps I brushed my teeth on Sunday mornings when I went to Congolese church with everyone else. But otherwise, my teeth were covered with layers of yellow gunk that I scraped off with my fingernails when I was bored in class.

This time, the dentist found six cavities. The prospect of getting all six of them drilled with no anesthesia made my heart sink. That afternoon after my checkup, I was swinging upside down like a monkey on the poles by the chapel with my brother Perry. I told him sadly that the dentist had found six cavities that morning.

Perry stood up and thrust his chest out proudly, saying, "Six? That's nothing! I have *nine* cavities!" Once again, my brother won the competition.

Gaboon Viper

Uncle Bill managed the building maintenance at Central School. When anything was broken, he fixed it. He also enjoyed making us laugh.

Uncle Bill was happy to be in Africa where he could hunt crocodiles. One day he shot one and cut it open. Inside he found a shirt, pants, and a pair of shoes. The villagers recognized the clothing of a man who had disappeared a few days earlier.

One Saturday, Uncle Bill brought home large crocodile

eggs for the children. He showed us how to preserve the egg by putting a small hole on each end, blowing the yoke out of the middle, and letting it dry in the sun. I kept my crocodile egg for a very long time.

One morning I was walking from English class to the library. Uncle Bill stood near the far wall of the building. He said, "Ruth, come here." Thinking this was one of his jokes, I said, "No, you're just teasing me, Uncle Bill."

He said a bit more urgently, "No, I'm not, Ruth. You need to come here quickly."

"Nah, stop teasing me, Uncle Bill."

"Then look behind you and don't step back." I looked down at the sidewalk. One foot away was a thick snake slithering in my direction, his split tongue sliding in and out of his daggered mouth. I stepped forward quickly just in time as he kept gliding along. Soon other children and teachers gathered to watch this snake from a distance.

One of those teachers was Uncle Sid, our math and science teacher. He was stocky with reddish blond, crew cut hair. Uncle Sid could be kind if you stuck to the rules but could suddenly become angry if you broke them. On Saturday evenings he brought out his guitar to sing folk songs and tell us scary stories.

On this particular morning, Uncle Sid was ready with a long stick with a noose at the end. He let the snake move into the noose and quickly jerked the string to capture it around the neck. He had a large pickle jar filled with formaldehyde at the ready. He threw the violently squirming snake into the jar and quickly closed the lid. We gathered around and watched in wonder as the snake struggled inside the jar but soon came to rest.

On closer inspection, Uncle Sid concluded it was a Gaboon viper, the most poisonous snake in the world with 2-inch fangs. This viper-in-a-jar took a prominent place on the shelf in Uncle Sid's classroom. I could see it every day when I walked into science or math class, a daily reminder of my close brush with death.

Many years later, my husband and I took our children to a reptile house in Savannah, Georgia. It was filled with displays of live venomous and exotic snakes. One of the placards described what it was like to die from the bite of a Gaboon viper: "The person goes into a coma within an hour and is dead after only two hours. It's a peaceful and quick death."

That evening at dinnertime, Aunt Peggy gave the meal blessing, thanking God for protecting me from the Gaboon viper.

7

Gasoline Soup and Other Frugalities

It's a good thing I was taught to put little stock in material things and accept inconveniences as they come along. Otherwise I may not have enjoyed everyday life growing up in Congo.

Grandma King's Juicy Fruit Gum

"Hey, Ruth!" Mom called. "Come to the kitchen. You have a package from Grandma King." I ripped the brown paper off the package with Grandma's handwriting and peered inside the small box she had sent just for me. There was a bright yellow packet of Juicy Fruit gum. I hadn't seen one of those for three years.

"Maybe you can take it next week when you go to boarding school," Mom said. "If you chew just a half stick at a time, you can make it last a very long time." I carefully placed my brand-new pack of gum in a special pouch in my suitcase.

When I got to boarding school at Lubondai for fourth grade, I split a piece in half and chewed it all day long. I stuck it to my bed post that night and chewed it the next day. I repeated this practice for three days. By the end of the third day it turned into crumbs in my mouth. So I swallowed it bit by bit until it was all gone.

One day I decided to break out a new half stick of Juicy Fruit gum just before morning class. I relished the sweet taste in my mouth. I enjoyed my half stick of gum for the first hour of Aunt Phyllis's English class.

Then it was French class with Tante Bette. I sat at the back of the room minding my own business, enjoying the sweet, fresh taste of Juicy Fruit gum.

"Ruth, do you have gum in your mouth?" Tante Bette was standing at the chalk board glaring in my direction, chalk in hand.

"Oui, Madame," I said with a sinking heart.

"Well, you should know you're not allowed to chew gum in class. Come to the front of the room and throw it away."

I walked slowly to the front of the class, feeling the eyes of my classmates on the back of my head. There was no way I was going to throw out a brand-new half stick of Juicy Fruit gum from Grandma King.

Behind the cover of the teacher's desk, I bent way down over the waste basket. I took the gum out of my mouth, put it behind my ear, covered it with my short blonde hair, and walked back to my seat.

"Ruth, did you throw that gum away?" Tante Bette asked, her eyes boring into mine.

"No, Madame." I couldn't lie.

"Then go back to the waste basket and throw it away this time."

So I did.

I had a hard time forgiving Tante Bette for making me throw away a brand new perfectly delicious half stick of Juicy Fruit gum from Grandma King.

Mushy Green Beans

Before we left Flanagan for Kananga in 1962, there must have been a big sale on fresh green beans. Mom and Grandma King got the idea we should fill three barrels with canned green beans to last four years in Congo. I'm not sure why it was necessary to have green beans for lunch and dinner when plenty of iron-rich cassava greens were available in Congo.

I was required to eat at least two of these mushy, dull-green beans every time they were served in hopes that I would get used to the taste. I hid one under my plate and threw the second one under my chair. The trick was to make these mushy beans disappear before we cleared the table after supper. I wasn't very successful with this disappearing act.

Eudene and friend canning green beans

Mom made me eat the one under my plate before I left the table. She usually didn't notice the bean under my chair until the table was cleared and we had all left the dining room.

Lake Munkamba

Camping in Congo

We enjoyed camping as a family at Lake Munkamba that was about a six-hour drive from Kananga. We wanted to jump into the lake as soon as we arrived, but Dad called us back to get everything unloaded and the campsite set up before anyone could play.

There were no carefully manicured campsites with fire pits in Congo. We created our own campsite under the big mango tree or in the rubble of someone's vacation home destroyed during the rebellion.

Priscilla does her laundry at Lake Munkamba

Mom set up her kitchen on a foldout metal table next to the campfire, with a few pans she'd brought from home. Dad set up his office with his typewriter on a small table under the tree.

Paul, Perry, Eudene fixing dinner at Lake Munkamba

We had devotions every night by kerosene lamplight. The girls slept in the book mobile; the guys slept on cots under mosquito nets outside.

Evening Devotions at Lake Munkamba

We learned to watch out for snakes on the walls of destroyed buildings, curled under Dad's desk, or nested along the edge of the lake while we were swimming.

Gasoline Soup

When I was in high school in 1972, there was a worldwide gasoline shortage. Gas lines in the United States went around the block. In Kinshasa, gas lines went for at least a mile down the street.

For two days and two nights, Uncle Earl and Uncle Mel took turns waiting to get gas at the pump station a couple blocks from the hostel. As a sophomore living in the Mennonite hostel with other kids in Kinshasa, I took my turn walking to the gas station to feed them at mealtime as they waited in line. We were part of the mission to fill the gas tank too. After all, the hostel bus had a big gas tank. The two men often came back with many stories after spending a full night or two at the pump.

When I went home to Kalonda that summer, Uncle Sam was preparing to take the three-day road trip in the big truck to Kananga to shop for food and supplies for the missionaries. Mom carefully put together our food order. She knew we would be charged not only for the food but also for the transport and gas expenses at this time of gas shortage. For some reason, we really needed those packaged soups and saltine crackers.

Uncle Sam left early one morning with a couple of PAX

guys. They were volunteers with Mennonite Central Committee on alternative service from the military. They went along with Uncle Sam to help drive the three-day journey to Kananga in the big red truck over bumpy roads with everyone's food order onboard.

Ten days later, Sam and the PAX guys returned. There was good news and bad news. The good news was that Uncle Sam was able to purchase nearly everything on our list. The bad news was that a barrel of gasoline had tipped over on the bumpy ride back and spilled gas all over our food. That wasn't a problem if the food was canned. But it was a problem for the packaged soups and saltine crackers that Mom had ordered in a very large quantity. And because a whole barrel of gas had spilled, the cost of that barrel had to be charged on top of the food order to make up for the loss.

That summer we ate a lot of gasoline soup for lunch. At 12:00 noon sharp, Mom came home from the maternity ward behind our house, and Dad came home from his literature office on the other side of Kalonda Station. I stepped away from the piano or put down my sewing project, and the three of us gathered at the lunch table.

The smell of gasoline-tomato or gasoline-chicken soup wafted through the house. Mom and Dad sipped the soup as though nothing was amiss. I complained a couple of times. But Dad said, "We can't throw all this soup away. We paid so much to get it here."

So we continued to eat gasoline soup every day that

summer until it was finally gone. We didn't waste a single package. Perhaps I can blame any lack of intelligence on a summer diet of gasoline soup.

The Bare Christmas Tree

In 1972, Mom went to the United States to be at brother Paul's wedding, leaving Dad and me alone for Christmas. I missed having Mom around while I was home from Kinshasa for the holiday.

Dad tried to make life interesting while Mom was away. He fixed oatmeal every morning for us to eat together. Then he puttered off on the yellow Honda 90 to his office on the other side of the station. Although he tried repeatedly, Dad never did get the hang of baking bread.

Levi's burnt bread

After Dad was done with work for the day, we walked down the steep hill through the tall, scratchy grass on a dirt path to the Kasai River in the valley below.

Swimming in the Kasai River

On our way back from the river a few days before Christmas, Dad said, "Let's get a Christmas tree to decorate in the living room." We kept an eye out for something suitable, but nothing looked quite like a Christmas tree. Finally, we decided to cut a branch off a Flamboyant tree, its many tiny leaves providing full foliage. We brought it home, put it into a bucket of dirt and decorated it for Christmas.

On Christmas Eve I came down with another bout of malaria. My fever spiked to 103 degrees Fahrenheit. I felt lethargic and decided to sleep on the couch to admire the tree. I missed Mom's nursing attention.

On Christmas morning I woke up to see that all the tiny leaves had fallen off the tree and were scattered all over the living room floor. The branches were totally bare, though the decorations were still intact. Our Christmas presents were covered with a million tiny leaves.

Dad came out of his bedroom and glanced at the bare tree. "Well at least we each have two presents to open this morning." He swept up the leaves and cooked our oatmeal for Christmas breakfast. He missed Mom too.

My Homemade Judo Jacket

In my second semester of my senior year, I took a judo class with my closest friends. I was excited about this special, small gym class with the more individualized attention from our coach.

We each had to make our own judo jacket. Mom was visiting Kinshasa at the time and offered to help. She found an old white sheet. We looked at pictures of judo outfits and sewed the outfit together.

I proudly wore my judo outfit to gym class the next day, along with the others. Coach said, "Okay, everybody, line up along the mat so I can test out your judo outfits."

One by one he grabbed each girl's judo top by the lapel.

All the girls took the judo stance, and Coach threw down each girl who made a loud slap on the mat with her arm. Fortunately, we had already learned how to fall safely. One by one, the girls' judo outfits took the sudden tug at the lapel.

Coach came to me and held my lapel. I was ready for that judo fall. Rrriip! To my great embarrassment, my brand-new judo top made from a cheap sheet ripped in two. I was glad I had a T-shirt underneath.

"Well, I guess you'll have to make another judo outfit, Ruth, with better quality fabric. Get it done by tomorrow."

Adibas Shoes

After college I returned to Kinshasa to work in the same hostel where I had attended high school. As a young adult living in Kinshasa, I enjoyed jogging along the Congo River outside the city in the late afternoon. I took long runs on Saturday mornings. The road had little traffic and followed along the curves of the fast-flowing river. I ran past the president's lion's cage on the corner, jogged a couple more miles to the beginning of the rapids, turned around, and ran back home.

But I needed some new running shoes. Someone was going to town, so I hitched a ride. I hadn't bought a new pair of running shoes for several years.

The shoe stores were right outside the Grand Marche. A Pakistani merchant pointed to a pair high on the shelf with some shiny, brown Adidas shoes, insignia and all. They were only $10. Sold!

I loved wearing my Adidas shoes, eagerly putting them on before every run. But after a short time I noticed the leather was quickly becoming brittle, and the shoes were causing blisters on my feet.

About two weeks later, my friend said, "Hey, didn't you notice the insignia says Adi*b*as, not Adi*d*as." Sadly, I realized I had bought counterfeit shoes.

"Oh well, this is Kinshasa," I thought. "No way I'm going to get my money back." So I continued to wear my Adibas shoes as long as I could stand them.

Roots of Frugality

Our family's commitment to frugality and making do with what we had came from a variety of sources. My parents both grew up on a farm during the Great Depression when they learned to live with less, as many did in their generation. My husband Jonathan's parents grew up with similar frugal sensibilities from the Depression. When I ask Jonathan for a piece of Scotch tape, he asks, "Do you want an Edgar size (half inch) or a Levi size (quarter inch) of tape?"

Coming from the Mennonite tradition, a simple lifestyle is an integral part of our faith. We're taught to be grateful for what we have and to share our resources with others.

Living as missionaries in Central Africa, a simple lifestyle was necessary. We couldn't drive to the nearest supermarket to get what we needed at the drop of a hat.

My husband and I tried to practice frugality as we raised our four children, sometimes to their chagrin. Instead of purchasing the latest Halloween costume, our children created their own from the dress-up box in the basement. We kept a cupboard full of school supplies to use instead of purchasing new supplies each time. There were notebooks that weren't used up yet, pens and pencils that were still useful, and erasers and pencil sharpeners that were still workable. Instead of getting the latest Nintendo, we took them to the library to get a box of books every weekend.

Being frugal has made it easier for me to live and travel overseas, sleeping in less-than-optimal settings, enjoying the food set on the table in front of me, saving money by purchasing clothing at the thrift shop, and serving as the barber for our entire family.

8

The President's Daughter's Wedding

"The President of the Republic of Zaire and Mama Bobi Ladawa are happy for you to share in the marriage of their daughter Mobutu Ngombo Toku, with Bossekota w'Atshia." As a member of the church council at the International Protestant Church of Kinshasa, I was honored to receive this invitation in 1981.

I had returned to Kinshasa after college to work as a hostel parent at the Mennonite hostel for missionary children where I lived in high school. After two years, I spent three years with the Mennonite Central Committee as administrative assistant for the country office.

I'd heard rumors that President Mobutu was spending an exorbitant amount of money on his daughter's wedding. Would I be showing support for his corrupt financial policies by attending? It didn't take me too long to decide that I'd go anyway. After all, how often does someone get the opportunity to attend the wedding of a president's daughter?

This occasion took place in the Palais du Peuple, a gift to Mobutu from the Chinese government. We entered the ballroom-sized foyer. Several chandeliers hung across the length of the high ceiling. Two large staircases rose on either side of the ballroom like a Cinderella movie. Staff were setting up bars for the reception and rolling out red carpets for the arrival of the President, the bride, and her entourage.

After we found our seats in the balcony, we walked around to the large windows on the second floor that looked out on the arrival area below. Lavish fountains had been turned on. Bands and dance groups were spaced around the sprawling square to greet the wedding party.

Soon we heard sirens in the distance. Along the driveway, guards dressed in green uniforms and large black hats stood at attention with their bayonets. Police cars with sirens and flashing lights escorted two large black limousines to the front door below us. Two Jeeps mounted with machine guns accompanied the cavalcade in front and back.

The entourage was whisked inside, passing directly beneath us. We watched President Mobutu and his daughter move through the foyer, and then we hurried back to our seats to watch them come down the aisle of the auditorium.

Four choirs sang during the ceremony. The gist of the sermon was this: "In these days when so many marriages are falling apart, there is only one way a couple can have a happy marriage and remain faithful to each other. That is if the marriage is centered around Jesus Christ." We wished the best for them.

After the ceremony, we rushed back onto the second-floor foyer to beat the crowd. The bridal party went to an elevator and came up to the second floor, stepping out about 20 feet in front of us.

We followed closely behind and came to a quiet, richly decorated sitting room complete with chandeliers, candles, and Persian rugs. The bride and groom sat on a couch and posed for pictures while the rest of the bridal party sat down on lounge chairs placed around the room.

President Mobutu sat about three feet away from where we were standing against the wall. He told his youngest daughter to look at the cameras and smile. The twenty photographers were more interested in taking pictures of Mobutu than they were of the bride and groom.

We left the wedding party and made our way down the ballroom stairs to the foyer where the reception was in progress. The scene in the foyer wasn't nearly as quiet and orderly as the scene we had just left.

There had been a mad rush to the lavish food so carefully displayed. Some guests tore large chunks of meat off the chicken or lamb with their bare hands. Some stuffed sandwiches into their pockets, baskets, and handkerchiefs. Others carried entire carcasses of turkey, lamb, and duck out of the building. Someone poured beer over another person's hands to wash them, and beer spilled onto the shiny, white-tiled floor.

Very soon the only food left were sandwich rolls minus the meat and cheese. The floor was a mushy mess with fragments of food and spilled beer. Fortunately, the food tables and bars were set apart from the plush red carpets as if the palace staff had foreseen what could take place.

The paradox was overwhelming. We knew what we were seeing was the natural reaction of hungry people. Here we were in perhaps the swankiest palace in Congo attending a very expensive wedding of the President's daughter. The attendees scavenged without shame.

The scene brought us down to earth. After all, we were in Congo where people struggled to meet basic needs for survival.

When the wedding party finally came down the staircase, they seemed oblivious to the frenzied scene in the foyer. They were immediately surrounded by photographers and important diplomats who were waiting to congratulate the couple and shake hands with the President.

We were looking at two completely disparate worlds in one room. It made me wonder what it would take for the President to look down from his exalted position and show compassion for his own people. At that time, Mobutu Sese Seko Kuku Ngbendu Wa Za Banga was one of the richest men in the world, using Congo's natural minerals to build his own wealth. (8.1)

Mobutu gave himself that name in 1972. It translates to "the all-powerful warrior who, because of his endurance and inflexible will to win, will go from conquest to conquest, leaving fire in his wake." Here is another translation: "A rooster who leaves no hen unplucked."

Mobuto was finally ousted in 1997 by a rebellion of his own people after thirty-two years of hard rule. He lived the rest of his life in Morocco where he died of prostate cancer three months after he was exiled from Congo.

Return to Congo

By the time I went to college in Indiana, I had spent more than half of my life in Congo. I was an American yet felt very out of place in the United States. I had difficulty entering into conversations about entertainment or fashion. I sought friendships with others who had lived overseas, but those friends were few and far between. I found American culture to be materialistic and uninteresting. I often felt lonely and isolated.

John Franz (left) with hostel bus
outside the Mennonite Hostel in Kinshasa

At the same time, I wasn't Congolese. Yet Congo still felt like home four years after I left. I wanted to figure out why Congo still held such an emotional grip on me.

That's why I took the opportunity to return to Congo after college graduation to serve as a hostel parent in the Mennonite hostel in Kinshasa where I had attended high school. I thought I could be of service as someone who understood the missionary children, as one who had "been there." As it turned out, being a hostel parent was probably the most challenging placement I ever had in my life. I was only four years older than the oldest child resident. I wanted to be their best friend but was in a position of authority, which made friendship difficult.

Beginning My Journey with Mennonite Central Committee

Two years later at the age of twenty-five, I joined Mennonite Central Committee (MCC) in Kinshasa. This was the beginning of a long, satisfying journey with a community of people with common vision, values, and principles.

Joining MCC was also the beginning of my political awakening. In MCC we were encouraged to observe, analyze, and think critically about root causes of poverty and violence in ways I had never thought of before. Although I grew up in Congo, I hadn't paid much attention to how President Mobutu was raping his country of its natural resources for his own wealth. I began to look around me and recognize how this President was driving his people deeper into poverty through kleptocracy.

What a privilege it was to work in Congo as a young adult. I was allowed to learn new things about the country that I had missed growing up there as a child. As the MCC Congo administrative assistant, I learned how to manage complex logistics in an unpredictable and messy national infrastructure. I learned how to talk myself out of unjust police arrests and walk away with a high five and a handshake. I learned how to procure visas, ID cards, and passports through a seemingly impossible and irredeemable system. I learned about dogged determination in the face of discouraging results. I learned how to work a dysfunctional system and get things done that needed to be done for the sake of my MCC team.

Young Adult Support Group, Kinshasa 1982

And the most fun of all was enjoying a small community of other young adults. We were all going through a similar process of learning through our time together in Kinshasa. Many in this community were providing logistics for mission and service agencies as I was with MCC. We learned from each other's strategies, successes, and failures. We encouraged each other through support and long conversations. In 1978, we started a weekly young adult support group for expatriates in Kinshasa that continues to this day.

Many of these friends continued into service occupations as teachers, ministers, missionaries, and social workers. Kinshasa in many ways was a launching pad for service careers for these young adult friends.

9

Raising a Family Under Embargo

In August 1989, a Cambodian woman gave birth to a baby girl in Trapeang Kraloeng Village, Kampong Speu Province, Cambodia. The birth was difficult as evident from the child's damaged neck muscles. The mother likely gave birth in the village with the help of a traditional birth attendant. She died in childbirth as was all too common in Cambodia at that time. The baby was likely three weeks premature.

Several Cambodian factions were fighting along the border with Thailand. Many landmines were in the rice paddies ready to maim an unlucky farmer who might step in the wrong place. Many soldiers from all factions came from Kampong Speu Province where this child was born. Her birth father was likely one of those soldiers.

In 1989 there was famine in the area. Families sometimes sent their babies to the orphanage because they couldn't afford to feed them, even those whose mothers survived. This baby's mother didn't survive the birth, the father had probably been killed in battle, and the family couldn't afford to buy milk. So they took her to the provincial orphanage in Kampong Speu town. This provincial orphanage wasn't equipped to care for infants.

At the provincial orphanage, the baby continued to languish. They decided to send her to Phnom Penh in hopes that she would survive. The child didn't yet have a name as the custom was to wait until the child was one month old to be sure they first survived infancy.

Kang Kak, a family friend from her village, arrived with the baby girl at the Nutrition Center Orphanage in Phnom Penh on August 18, 1989. The family must have cared deeply for this child since they went to the effort and expense of sending her to Phnom Penh. So many babies whose mothers died in childbirth were not given this special attention. Kang registered the baby with Madame Chan Vaddey, the head mistress of the orphanage in Phnom Penh.

Madame Pok Oeurn was a loving nurse in the orphanage and took special care of the little girl like she was her own. She fed her slowly and regularly so she could digest the food properly through her underdeveloped digestive system.

But the little girl was weak and malnourished, not able to swallow properly or hold anything in her little belly. She continued to lose weight. At two weeks of age she weighed only four pounds. They brought her to Phnom Penh Hospital where the doctor saw her fighting survivor spirit and named her Yuth Neary, which means "young woman soldier."

Jonathan and I were married in 1988 and went to work for MCC in Cambodia six months later. One of the connecting points in our relationship was a desire to work and live abroad for a period. The opportunity to work as co-representatives for Mennonite Central Committee in Cambodia captured our imagination. My administrative experience and Jonathan's training and work as a pediatrician seemed to meet the needs at the time.

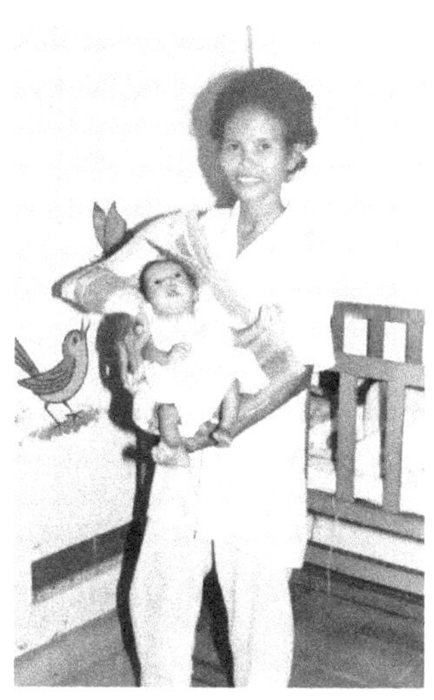

Yut Neary (Carla) with Pok Oeurn

We decided to adopt a baby in Cambodia. We were told by the Ministry of Foreign Affairs that we had to choose a child to adopt before we could begin the formal application process.

We knew it was risky to get attached to one child. No Americans had been allowed to adopt in Cambodia since before 1975, fourteen years earlier, when Cambodia fell to the Khmer Rouge. There was a good chance that as US citizens we would be refused for adoption by Cambodian authorities. After all, we came from the country that was leading the embargo from the West. From the Cambodian government's point of view, it would be a disgrace to allow one of the nation's children to become an American. But we were determined to take the risk anyway.

When Yuth Neary was three weeks old, we visited the orphanage to begin the process of choosing a baby to adopt. She had just returned from the hospital and was still having difficulty keeping her milk down. We visited the orphanage several times that first month in August 1989, always feeling a special tug toward Yuth Neary.

One morning, when Neary was one month old, I was sitting on a mat on the floor with several tiny babies and their nurse, Pok Oeurn.

"Have you decided yet to adopt one of our children?" she asked.

"Yes, we're considering adopting Yuth Neary. What do you think?"

Madame Oeurn let out a squeal and picked up the baby in her arms, gave her a big hug, and said, "What a lucky baby you are!"

"No, we will be the lucky ones," I replied.

We sent a letter to the Ministry of Foreign Affairs expressing our interest in adopting Neary. We pledged that she would be treated as one of our own. If we had more children, she would have an equal part of our inheritance. We promised that when she grew older, we would bring her back to Cambodia to get to know her cultural heritage. We would take her to visit the ancient temples of Angkor Watt, one of the seven manmade wonders of the world. Then we settled in for the long and arduous process, not realizing that the biggest hurdle would be our own U.S. government.

Ruth and Jonathan at Angkor Watt 1989

At that time, the Cambodian government was under a U.S. led embargo and not recognized as a legal government by most Western nations. Therefore, any legal documents from Cambodia were not recognized by the U.S. government.

We sent a letter to the American embassy in Bangkok, Thailand, to inform the U.S. authorities of our desire to adopt a Cambodian child. A couple of weeks later, we received the following response:

> I am sorry to inform you that at the present time there are no means by which you will be able to adopt a Khmer and proceed with the child to the United States. The process of adopting a child who is not a United States citizen can only be accomplished

> through the diplomatic mission in the child's country. The United States has no formal diplomatic relations with Cambodia at this time.

Neary, now renamed Carla, had already been in our home for a month since we had received permission from the Cambodian government. Were we going to return her to the orphanage? Absolutely not!

While we were waiting for permission to adopt Carla, Peter Jennings of *ABC News* walked into our apartment at the Samaki Hotel in February 1990. He asked if he could interview us about our experience as Americans living in Cambodia. We were giving Carla her first feeding of rice porridge, and Peter held her on his lap to get acquainted. We were pleased to be featured in a short clip of his documentary, *Peter Jennings Reporting from the Killing Fields*. (9.1)

Gratefully, after many letters and petitions, we were able to get a visa for Carla to come to the United States for adoption proceedings a year later. That was possible through many personal acquaintances and friends, including the U.S. Consulate in Laos that advocated on our behalf.

Punishing a Post-Genocidal Society

In 1979, Cambodia was left flat on its back after four years of the disastrous rule of Pol Pot's Khmer Rouge. During that regime, an estimated 20 percent of the population died of killings, starvation, and disease. The country's infrastructure was shattered and the population thoroughly traumatized. Most Cambodian people with some professional training had either died or fled to the Thai border. (9.2)

Jonathan at Toul Sleng, Khmer Rouge prison in Phnom Penh

At the same time, Cambodia was subjected to an intense US-led international embargo on aid and commerce through most of the 1980s and into the early 1990s as a way to punish Vietnam, which was backing the Cambodian government. Simultaneously, three other factions were fighting against the Cambodian regime. Thousands of Cambodians languished in refugee camps along the Thai-Cambodian border.

Testing a typewriter donated by MCC to the Ministry of Education

In the early 1990s when we asked young people what their plans were for the future, we hoped to hear about potential studies, getting married, pursuing a career, and so on. But most often their response was this: “How can I plan even for next year? I don't know whether there will be war or peace. I'm not sure I'll have a job to support myself, much less a family. I need to take it a day at a time and not get my hopes up for the future."

MCC Country Representatives in Cambodia

From 1988 to 1993, Jonathan and I were country representatives in Cambodia for Mennonite Central Committee (MCC), the relief, development, and peacebuilding organization for Mennonite and Brethren in Christ churches in the United States and Canada. Because the embargo prevented a large influx of humanitarian assistance, our small non-governmental organization (NGO) defied the U.S. led embargo by working through Canadian banks, providing much-needed development aid to the country.

Purchasing fruit on a street corner of Phnom Penh

Jonathan and I left for Cambodia in November 1988, just six months after we were married. We were adjusting to married life and Cambodian life, working closely together as co-representatives and wanting to start a family in our early thirties. It was a lot to ask of ourselves and our young marriage. But we were ready for it.

Our role was to manage funding and personnel for MCC's community development projects. Together we supported a team of American, Canadian, Indian, and Cambodian physicians, nurses, irrigation engineers, and community development workers.

Jonathan working with doctors
at Neak Luong Hospital

By the time the Khmer Rouge was ousted from Cambodia in 1979, there was only a handful of doctors left in the country. The medical system had to be totally rebuilt and new physicians trained. Jonathan monitored MCC's support of health systems in Prey Veng Province. He made weekly trips to Neak Luong Hospital to work directly with the physicians.

When MCC began to work in Cambodia in 1982, rebuilding Neak Luong Hospital was one of its first projects. Strengthening this hospital was not only essential for health care in Prey Veng Province, but it was also deeply symbolic for an American NGO to rebuild the hospital that had been destroyed by U.S. bombing in 1972 during President Richard Nixon's secret war on Cambodia. (9.3) The bombing of Neak Luong Hospital is what made the American people aware of the secret bombing of Cambodia. That led to student protests at Kent State University and the death of four students after being shot by the National Guard.

For five years, Jonathan was out of the medical milieu in the United States. Some of our acquaintances questioned whether it was wise for him to leave mainstream medical practice for this assignment in Cambodia. Wasn't he going to lose out on opportunities to advance as a medical professional?

In fact, this time in Cambodia gave him a more holistic view of the practice of medicine, making him a more well-rounded physician with a public health orientation. It helped him tune in to the social contexts of his patients. The Cambodian experience gave him a sense of purpose through developing himself as a person, opening his worldview and enhancing his care for patients who are immigrants in the United States.

Embargoed Communications

In the meantime, in August 1990, I delivered our second child, Christopher, in Bangkok. This was an unexpectedly early delivery after a long flight from Phnom Penh through Ho Chi Minh City, Vietnam, to Bangkok. I flew out a month before my due date. Jonathan was planning to come two weeks later with Carla.

I arrived at the Bangkok Christian Guest House late that night. I unpacked my suitcase and set up my laptop, eager to get some solid work done during the next month. August was the time of year to work on project proposals and reports for MCC.

Soon after I went to bed, my water broke. Everyone in the guest house had already gone to bed. The Thai receptionist ran out to the street and hailed a taxi to take me to the hospital. My contractions started while I was riding alone in the taxi. Gratefully, the hospital was only a half hour drive away with little traffic at midnight.

Because I arrived late at night, I hadn't had a chance to get funds at the MCC office that day to give Samitivej Hospital a down payment for admission. So I gave them my passport to hold as a guarantee that I would pay after the baby was born.

After only five hours of labor, Dr. Nisarat, whom I had met only once before, delivered Christopher one month before his due date.

I was eager to let Jonathan know that the baby had been born upon my arrival. But because Thailand was also part of the embargo against Cambodia, communication between the two countries wasn't yet well developed.

We didn't have a phone connection in our home, so it was impossible to call him. I sent him a telegram, but he didn't receive it.

The director of Handicap International who was visiting Bangkok at the time sent a message to her staff in Phnom Penh to notify Jonathan. The message didn't get through.

I sent Jonathan a telex (before the fax era). Unfortunately, the only hotel that had a telex machine in Phnom Penh hadn't yet developed their delivery system. So the telex message sat in the Hotel Cambodiana office for several days until the Director of World Food Program in Cambodia stumbled upon it while he was looking for his own.

Thankfully, this director went to our apartment and knocked on Jonathan's door to let him know there was a telex waiting for him at the hotel and that he might want to see it.

Once Jonathan retrieved the telex one week after Christopher's birth, he started to make quick arrangements to fly to Thailand. At the time there were no direct flights from Phnom Penh to Bangkok because of the embargo, and the weekly flight to Ho Chi Minh City, Vietnam, had just departed that morning.

Ta Yon, our driver and logistics coordinator, quickly took a letter to the Ministry of Foreign Affairs asking permission for Jonathan and Carla to go to Vietnam overland

and catch the flight to Bangkok from Ho Chi Minh City as soon as possible. He quickly got a visa for Jonathan to enter Vietnam.

Because Carla's passport was from the Cambodian government (Hun Sen regime), she wasn't allowed entry into Thailand without special permission. If she had had a Khmer Rouge passport, the Thai government would have allowed her entry.

The MCC secretary in Bangkok called the Thai Ministry of Foreign Affairs, pleading for permission to allow Carla entry into Thailand with her father for emergency humanitarian purposes. One week after Chris was born, Jonathan finally met his one-week-old son in the lobby of the Bangkok airport. Gratefully, Carla was with him.

We soon discovered that Dr. Bopha, Chris's Thai pediatrician, had done her medical residency at the Mennonite Hospital in Bloomington where she had been precepted by my grandparents' doctor. It was a "small world" gift.

By the time Andy was born in December 1991 in Bangkok, life was a bit simpler. Peace talks were in full swing, and the embargo was about to be lifted. Carla had been officially adopted in Lancaster, Pennsylvania, and had an American passport. Travel was much easier for the entire family to go to Thailand and the United States. The only hitch with Andy's birth was that Dr. Nisarat had just left the hospital and got caught in Bangkok traffic, so she didn't make it back in time for the delivery.

A Front-Row Seat

During this five-year period in Cambodia, we had the opportunity to observe firsthand a dramatic societal shift. We arrived ten years after the Khmer Rouge had been ousted from Cambodia in 1979. It was a post-genocidal society. Everyone had a story of loss and death under the Khmer Rouge.

When we arrived in 1988, we lived under a strict Marxist-Leninist government with a centralized economy. The United States led an embargo from most Western countries. After a complex series of peace talks, we witnessed the return of their exiled King Sihanouk as his motorcade rode past our house.

The embargo was lifted in 1992, which led to a year of the largest-ever UN presence. Twenty-two thousand soldiers—the UN Transitional Authority in Cambodia (UNTAC)—from all over the world descended on Cambodia. The second-largest-ever UN presence was in Congo in 1960 when my family evacuated (see Chapter 2). UNTAC prepared the Cambodian people for the first multi-party elections they had had since 1955. We observed this election in August 1993 when large, expectant crowds lined up at multiple polling stations around Phnom Penh and beyond, their colorful umbrellas shading them from the brilliant sun. During those five years from 1988 to 1993, Cambodia had gone through four different flags to represent each shift of government.

Before 1993, Cambodian NGOs were not allowed to

exist. One of our most satisfying endeavors as MCC representatives was to give the first seed grant to a local Cambodian NGO that was emerging toward the end of our five-year term. This NGO encouraged youth to discuss healthy relationships and peaceful conflict resolution. That NGO continues to thrive today, contributing to civil society and peacebuilding throughout the country. MCC has been supporting peacebuilding NGOs in Cambodia now for many years. Our son Christopher served for one year with one of these NGOs.

Providing leadership to the MCC team in Cambodia during those unique five years was deeply satisfying despite many frustrations of working under embargo. We sensed that we were part of something bigger, advocating for more international attention to the plight of the Cambodians. We managed the transition from a big fish in a little pond (being one of very few NGOs during the embargo) to a small fish in a big pond (when Cambodia opened up to the world of the UN and multilateral aid). That gave us an opportunity to implement a vision for MCC to engage with emerging local NGOs that wanted to build a peaceful civil society.

Coming Full Circle

Hana was born in Baltimore in 1996 to complete our family of six. In June 2011, we took our four children back to Cambodia for a visit. A primary goal was to give Carla, then a college graduate, the opportunity to explore her birth roots. We traveled to her birth village and talked with mothers who had delivered children at the same time as her birth. As we had promised at her adoption, we took the family to visit the ancient temples of Angkor Watt.

We found Pok Oeurn, Carla's nurse who had cared for her during the first three months of her life. Oeurn expressed deep gratitude that we had taken the time to find her. We were grateful for her time and conversation with Carla, the baby she had cared for so lovingly who was now a grown young woman.

Carla, Pok Oeurn and Ruth

Cambodia continues to live in our hearts as a key touchstone experience of the beginning of our family life. Although our children don't remember much of that time early in their lives, it strengthened our family's understanding that we are part of something much bigger than our own little family community. This foundational time has encouraged each of us to pursue careers that serve the community beyond ourselves.

Chris, Hana, Andy, Carla, Jonathan, Ruth,
at Angkor Watt in 2011

10

What Is Your Function?

Only fifteen American citizens lived in Cambodia when Jonathan and I arrived in 1988 due to the US-led embargo from the West. Cambodians were totally isolated from the outside world. During those first two years of our term, Cambodians were not allowed to fraternize with Westerners and were closely watched by spies from the Ministry of Interior. Yet young people were eager to relate to Westerners in whatever way they could without getting caught.

There was a street in Phnom Penh called English Street. It was lined with signs that said, "Essential English, Book One taught here," "Essential English Book Two," or "Come here for best English class." Usually the Cambodian teachers were barely one lesson ahead of their students. Many Cambodian young people flocked to this street to learn English as a bridge to the outside world.

We found that the best way to develop friendships with

Cambodians in those years of embargo was to bike to the Olympic Stadium every afternoon after work to jog around the track. On our way, young men rode their bicycles alongside us to try out their English. Perhaps they thought they would be less likely to get caught by spies if they rode their bikes or jogged next to us.

The conversation usually went something like this:

"Hello!"

"Hello!"

"What is your name?"

"My name is Ruth."

And invariably the next question was this: "What is your function?"

What is your function? What did that question mean?

It took us a while to realize they were simply practicing their first English lesson in "Essential English Book One."

We were never quite sure what that question meant. "What is your function?" But we thought it was a good question.

Since then, I have often asked myself that question: "What is my function?" or "What is my mission?" "What is my purpose in life?"

Ruth at Zongo Falls

Recognizing My Privilege

Recognizing my privilege has been an important part of my journey toward understanding my purpose in the world. I was born into privilege, a Caucasian who never experienced racism, a U.S. citizen who could return to the stability of this country when things got dicey elsewhere. I was given the opportunity to have an education and travel and learn from the world even as a young child. I've been allowed to enjoy good health.

Destruction in Aleppo Syria

I became aware of my privilege when I traveled to Irbil, Iraq, in 2014, soon after 50,000 people were driven out of Mosul by ISIS and had walked 50 miles to safety. These internally displaced refugees were living in crowded church basements and school classrooms. Family units were divided by thin curtains for privacy. One woman, when seeing us approach her humble abode, said, "We don't want your sympathy; we just want to go home."

I again became acutely aware of my privilege while traveling in Syria in 2018 as International Program Director for Mennonite Central Committee. This trip took place in 2018 at the height of the war in Syria. Driving through Homs and Aleppo, we saw large buildings of destroyed concrete piled high with seemingly no chance of reconstruction. It reminded me of pictures from post–World War II Europe. We drove through miles and miles of abandoned villages with no signs of life.

We heard heartbreaking stories from elderly mothers and fathers of losing sons to war or kidnapping, or a daughter who had migrated to Europe with her husband to avoid the draft. Aging parents didn't know who would care for them when they grew old.

Visiting internally displaced families in the Qalamoun Valley

Those we visited expressed gratitude that we would risk visiting them in Syria during the war, letting them know the world was paying attention to their plight.

I came home to Baltimore and decorated my house for Christmas. All four of our young adult children came home to celebrate Christmas with us. I didn't have to wonder where my children were.

So I've had to ask myself how I can practice gratitude and generosity, using my privilege for the betterment of others.

Finding My Purpose in Leadership

During my senior year of high school in Kinshasa, our youth sponsor had invited me to her home one Saturday morning to talk. She said she observed the times I had taken on leadership roles in the youth group and wondered if God was calling me to use my gifts in the broader church. She talked about the joys and challenges of being a leader and wondered if I would be ready to accept such a responsibility. I took her challenge seriously.

Through various opportunities in MCC, I learned that collaborative leadership is the most effective way to accomplish anything—bringing people onboard from the beginning, hearing others' ideas, brainstorming together, encouraging outside-the-box thinking, and being open to the possibility that others may have better ideas than mine.

During my work with MCC, I met inspiring people from around the world who showed me ways to find purpose even through challenges. These colleagues and friends represent a global community who are committed to addressing the needs in their own settings and beyond. They live out their mission in life, aware of the big picture outside of themselves.

Academic Women Find Purpose in Iran

I traveled with an MCC delegation to Iran in 2014 to visit with Shia Muslim religious leaders. This was an opportunity to engage in inter-religious dialogue and compare teachings on peacebuilding between Mennonites and Shia Muslims.

The women of our group wore long, black gowns, making sure no hair peeked out of our head coverings. When entering a holy place, the women went through one door and the men through another.

We visited the large women's Alzahara University and observed the rich, intellectual life of academic Shia women. We observed their gentle and joyful demeanor as they found meaning and purpose in their own rich community of women.

Young Adults Find Purpose in War-Torn Syria

While traveling in Syria, we met hundreds of young adults who had been trained by MCC to respond to the internally displaced in their own communities. They enthusiastically fed people, provided safe housing, and conducted peacebuilding workshops through grants provided by MCC.

We asked a group of young adults in Damascus why they chose to volunteer in this way. One of them said, "When we have children, they will ask what we were doing during this time of war in Syria. We want to be able to tell them that we were helping others."

Mothers Find Purpose in Eastern Congo

Eastern Congo is one of the most beautiful places in the world, with lush forests, volcanoes, and mountains dotting the landscape. Its beauty belies the tragedy that continues to unfold in the land. This part of Congo has experienced ongoing civil war since 1996 with over six million lives lost and millions still displaced.

I met a mother outside of Goma who fled from her home with her six children when the M23 rebels invaded her village. She did not know where her husband was.

This family was living with other internally displaced neighbors in a school while waiting for food and assistance. This woman was strong and determined to protect and provide for her family even without the support of her husband. To me, she was symbolic of the many women in Congo who provide for their families in the absence of their husbands due to war. In the midst of this chaos, she found purpose.

Youth Find Purpose Through Peacebuilding in Cambodia

Suyheang Kry is the director of Women Peace Makers, an NGO active throughout Cambodia. She brings together youth from a variety of ethnicities—Khmer, Vietnamese, Cham, Thai—to build understanding and peace across ethnic divides.

Peace Club in Cambodia

When I visited Cambodia in 2019, Suyheang told me that instead of marrying young as her family expected, she chose to go to school and continue her college education so she could have a long-term impact on the youth of Cambodia.

We attended one of the many peace clubs that have grown out of Women Peace Makers. Youth from across the cultural and religious spectrum in Cambodia gathered to play games, act out conflict scenarios through theater, and engage in vigorous debate on how to maintain peace in their communities through differences. By practicing her mission with youth in Cambodia, Suyheang has enabled the youth to practice theirs by bringing peace to their communities.

A Pastor Finds Purpose Practicing Nonviolence in Colombia

I visited a community rice-processing plant in the Chocó region of Colombia that was managed by the local Mennonite church. A heavily armed paramilitary group once pressured the church to pay a war contribution from this rice processing plant. But their Pastor Rivas responded firmly, "Mennonite churches have been committed to nonviolence and peacebuilding for centuries. We will not support any armed groups. If you force us, we will close this community development project, but we will not support you, even if it costs us our lives."

Surprised by this boldness and aware that Mennonites in Colombia have held this position throughout time, the paramilitary commander promised to respect his word. The community development work was able to continue. The pastor lived out his mission as a witness for nonviolence.

Asylum Seekers Find Purpose in Baltimore

North Baltimore Mennonite Church houses and supports asylum seekers at the Reservoir Hill House of Peace (RHHP).

Jonathan and I helped start this ministry in 2003. These resident asylum seekers fled their homes due to war, violence, and sometimes torture. They inevitably became targets on the wrong side of the political divide in their home countries. Some were imprisoned. Some were put into detention (prison) in the United States immediately after crossing the southern border. Yet I am often inspired by their sense of purpose and determination, pulling their lives together in the United States while overcoming countless barriers.

Reservoir Hill House of Peace

Kamba was a leader in the civil police force in his home country. He barely escaped two assassination attempts and had to flee to the United States for his own safety. Kamba finds purpose by providing quiet leadership where he lives in community at RHHP, bringing people together, planning events, and acting as mediator when there are disagreements among residents.

Surine finished medical school in Kabul when she had to leave Afghanistan due to the takeover of the Taliban. Being part of the Hazari minority group, her community was especially targeted as enemies of the majority group. As soon as she crossed the border into the United States, she and her sister were put into detention in Louisiana. I wrote a letter of sponsorship for their release, and they came to live at RHHP. They applied for asylum and a work permit as soon as they were allowed.

Once Surine got her work permit, she pursued a nurse's aide job and is now pursuing an undergraduate biology degree. Even though she's starting over, she is determined to become a doctor in the United States to fulfill her purpose in life.

Finding Purpose Through the Twists and Turns of Life

A friend once told me, "God is calling me to be a physical therapist in Texas, but I don't *want* to be a physical therapist in Texas." I had to wonder if God calls someone to something so specific without also giving them a sense of joy and anticipation as my mother had received as a nine-year-old.

I have come to believe that having a mission or purpose doesn't necessarily imply a particular place or profession. My life has taken many twists and turns, and times when I was uncertain of my direction.

Watching my parents live out their purpose in life with persistence and determination helped me trust life's outcomes that were sometimes beyond my control. Going through two rebellions in Congo helped me understand that living out a calling in life isn't always a straight shot. Unexpected detours along the journey are to be expected.

I experienced uncertainties as I struggled with American culture as a third-culture kid. I wasn't always sure if I fit in the United States or in Africa. There were times as a child and a young adult when I felt very alone and isolated in the world. But eventually I came to accept my "third-cultureness" as a gift. I realized that I didn't want to embrace the American way of life as the norm, that there were so many other rich cultures and ways to view the world that I could learn from outside my own. Having had the opportunity to live and travel to other parts of the world has given me a more global perspective on culture, politics, and life in general.

Reflections on the Congo River

It took me a while to decide on a college major. I settled on music and psychology, not because of a clear career direction but simply because I enjoyed both subjects. I later received a master's degree in counseling yet never became a licensed counselor. Was it a wasted degree? Much later I received a master's degree in management, which seemed to fit my interests. But it took a while to figure out what course of study was best for me.

I had always wanted to have children and am deeply grateful for the privilege of being a parent. My four children continue to teach me so much about life. But there were times when they were young that I wondered if I would ever get a chance to pursue a career. I sometimes forgot that there are seasons in life that come and go, seasons that are there to be celebrated.

The Evolution of Purpose

In many ways, my sense of purpose or mission wasn't always evident or straightforward. Rather it evolved from one engagement to the next, each stage of life preparing me for the next phase. Life has become more about curiosity, learning, and growth than about following a particular career path. I have learned to listen to my instincts as I pursue what it means to be part of something bigger than myself each step of the way.

For example, experiencing culture shock each time I returned to the United States gave me empathy for immigrants trying to find their way in this country. Going back to Congo as a young adult helped me integrate my upbringing with my adult life.

Living in Cambodia as a young parent under embargo

helped me appreciate the simple joys of family life. Being part of MCC opened many doors for international engagement and leadership.

During a time of unemployment and uncertainty, I had the space and opportunity to develop the Asylum Seekers Housing Network at the Reservoir Hill House of Peace. Working with asylum seekers in Baltimore has brought me great joy.

Choosing to Be Part of God's Big Story

I've chosen to enter what God is already doing in my community and in the world. God's mission is so much bigger than I am.

At the Mount of Olives, East Jerusalem

Having a purpose or mission does not imply that I will do great things by society's standards. We are here for the purpose of loving God, family, and neighbors, and to focus on the needs around us and in the world beyond.

I find my purpose by reflecting on life with gratitude and generosity, seeking ways to be part of God's big story with curiosity and expectancy.

Notes and References

P.1 *The Poisonwood Bible,* by Barbara Kingsolver, HarperCollins Publishers Inc, New York, NY. 1998

2.1 These stories of evacuation from Congo in 1960 were largely drawn from Levi Keidel's personal journals and the author's interviews with family members and missionaries.

2.2 *King Leopold's Ghost: A Story of Greed, Terror, and Heroism in Colonial Africa,* by Adam Hochschild, Houghton Mifflin Company, Boston and NY. 1998

2.3 *William Sheppard: Congo's African American Livingstone,* by William E. Phipps, Geneva Press, Louisville, KY. 2002

2.4 *CIM/AIMM: A Story of Vision, Commitment and Grace,* by Jim Bertsche, Fairway Press, Lima, OH. 1998

3.1 *Caught in the Crossfire,* by Levi Keidel, Herald Press, Scottdale, PA. 1979

4.1 Stories of Anna Holliger Keidel's experience of the 1918 Flu Pandemic are drawn from the author's interviews of her grandmother.

4.2 Stories of Levi Keidel's life are drawn from his personal journals.

5.1 *It's Been God's Doing All Along,* by Jim Bertsche, Africa Inter-Mennonite Mission, Elkhart, IN. 2012

8.1 *In the Footsteps of Mr. Kurtz: Living on the Brink of Disaster in Mobutu's Congo,* by Michela Wrong, Harper-Collins Publishers, Inc, New York, NY. 1998

9.1 "Peter Jennings Reporting: From the Killing Fields," ABC News Productions. 1990

9.2 *The Tragedy of Cambodian History: Politics, War, and Revolution Since 1945,* by David P. Chandler, Yale University Press, New Haven and London. 1991

9.3 *The Killing Fields,* British Biographical drama film directed by Roland Joffe, Screenplay by Bruce Robinson. Early scene depicts the American bombing of Neak Luong Hospital. 1984

About the Author

Ruth Keidel Clemens grew up in the Democratic Republic of Congo, where her parents served as Mennonite missionaries. She went on to serve with Mennonite Central Committee for 27 years in Congo, Cambodia, and the United States, holding a variety of leadership roles.

In 2020, Ruth created a website for young adults looking for practical tools to find their calling in life, at https://callingtools.net/. And in 2024, she published African Fables, Book III, a collection of stories her mother gathered from Congolese friends.

Ruth holds a B.S. in Music and Psychology from Indiana University (1978), an M.A. in Community Agency Counseling from Western Michigan University (1985), and an M.A. in Management from the College of Notre Dame in Maryland (1998).

She and her husband are active members of North Baltimore Mennonite Church, where Ruth plays piano and manages a house for asylum seekers. They live in Baltimore, Maryland, and have four adult children.

Discussion Questions

For adult formation, book clubs or personal reflection and journaling

Chapter 1 The Other Lakeshore

- Reflect on a significant turning point in your life. How did it change you? How have you shared that story with your family?
- Have you ever had a near death experience? How did it impact your outlook on life and your sense of purpose?

Chapter 2 Journey Out of Congo
Chapter 3 Praying Us Out of the Rebellion

- How do you justify the missionary endeavor with the requirement to work under the infrastructure of colonial authorities? How would you have navigated this dilemma?
- In what ways have you observed the impact of colonialism and imperialism, either in your own country or abroad?

- Reflect on the following scriptures. Do you think they imply personal, physical, or emotional protection? Community protection? Psalm 46:1-3; John 6:16-21; Hebrews 6:19; Psalm 91:1-4

Chapter 4 Developing Resiliency and Determination
Chapter 5 Where's Mom?

- What is your definition of resiliency?
- What life experiences have increased your resiliency? Was the pain worth the gain?
- What is your definition of "calling"? Do you think everyone has a calling, or is it only for the privileged? Is a calling individual, communal, or both?
- How have you experienced a sense of call in your life?

Chapter 6 A Nine-Year-Old Leaves Home
Chapter 7 Gasoline Soup and Other Frugalities

- Was there a time in your childhood when you were alone and had to make decisions on your own? How did that impact who you are today?
- What components of your family culture shaped you?
- How did a frugal life or a materially abundant life as a child shape you?

Chapter 8 The President's Daughter's Wedding

- Have you observed the disparate worlds of abject poverty and gross wealth in your own country or abroad? How has that experience reshaped your perspective?
- Have you found a community where you belong? What is it about that community that gives you a sense of belonging?
- What young adult experiences helped you find your calling?

Chapter 9 Raising a Family Under Embargo

- Have you ever had a goal you wanted to reach no matter what? What did you have to give up to reach that goal?
- Have you ever struggled to plan for your future? What obstacles stood in your way?
- How might the ability to plan ahead be a privilege?

Chapter 10 What Is Your Function?

- What are your privileges, and how do they impact your quality of life?
- Can you name a learning in one stage of life that prepared you for the next stage of life?
- When you're faced with a difficult time, what keeps you hopeful?

- How does the practice of gratitude impact your outlook on life?
- "We all have a place in God's mission in the world, wherever we are, in whatever we do." Do you believe this is true? How does "being part of God's mission in the world" look for you?

www.ingramcontent.com/pod-product-compliance
Lightning Source LLC
LaVergne TN
LVHW010622100826
845148LV00014B/3071

9781632969606